FEATURING POPULAR GARDENING IDEAS FROM
WALT DISNEY THEME PARKS & RESORTS

To obtain additional copies, contact:

Walt Disney Attractions
Guest Service/Mail Order
P.O. Box 10,070
Lake Buena Vista, FL 32830-0070
Phone: (800) 272-6201 or (407) 363-6200

or

Disneyland
Merchandise Guest Services
P.O. Box 3232
Anaheim, CA 92803
Phone: (800) 362-4533 or (714) 999-4216

First Edition
10 9 8 7 6 5 4 3 2 1

Written by Ann Groom
Designed by Dale Sprague & Kelly Mayhew
of Shields Design Group, Inc.
Illustrated by Cynthia Wooley, Lou Dellarosa & Jennifer Oliver
Inked by Mark Marderosian
Produced by Lee Ann Blystone

All rights reserved. No part of this book may be reproduced or utilized in any form or by any means, electronic or mechanical, including photocopying and recording, or by any information storage and retrieval system without express written permission from Walt Disney Attractions.

© The Walt Disney Company
Printed in U.S.A.

ACKNOWLEDGEMENTS

Special thanks to the Walt Disney World Resort
Horticulture Team and
Disneyland Resort Landscaping for
their valuable assistance and
expert guidance throughout the creation
of this book.

Contents

CASTLE

A red carpet of tulips brightly welcomes spring in Disneyland Park.

"I want something alive, something that can grow. Not only can I add things, but even the trees will keep growing. It will get more beautiful each year... And as I find out what the public likes... I can change it, because it's alive."

Walt Disney
Disneyland, 1955, Anaheim, California

This philosophy, combined with Walt's unwavering dedication to perfection, an unsurpassed creative genius, and dreams beyond compare, changed our lives in countless ways. Disneyland®, "the happiest place on earth," set new standards of quality in the world of entertainment and spawned the next generation of dreamers and doers. The astonishing success of Disneyland led to the Walt Disney World® Theme Parks and Resorts, Tokyo Disneyland® Park, and Disneyland® Paris.

The original Disneyland Park was to be a drastic departure from the old-time amusement parks and carnivals that catered mostly to children. Walt had grand visions of a place where children and parents, families and friends could all have fun together.

As Walt planned Disneyland in the early 1950s, he drew upon his early experience in the motion picture business and surrounded himself with a diversely talented team of artists, sculptors, designers, architects, engineers, storytellers, and special effects experts. Morgan "Bill" Evans, a man who eventually became known as the pioneering Disney landscape architect, was also by Walt's side during those early years. The group's duty, as Walt coined the term, was "imagineering."

These "imagineers" tackled the project as they would a motion picture. In film-making, telling the story consists of leading the audience through a series of events or "scenes." Transferring this principle to Disneyland, they determined that the audience (Disneyland guests) would actually experience the drama themselves. They would walk from "set to set," encountering and interacting with everything around them. To enhance the effect, it was agreed the landscape would be an integral element of the whole experience. Visitors would float along a mysterious river through a dense jungle, journey back in time to the deserts of the Old West, or marvel at fantasy, fairy-tale gardens.

The Landscape Show

The "show business" influence is evident in all the Walt Disney Theme Parks and Resorts, just as planned. Walt envisioned the landscapes as huge outdoor stages or sets with the trees, shrubs, flowers, and turf playing the roles of props as well as stars. He also wanted the entire spectacle to be in top form 365 days a year. To do this, it takes careful planning, meticulous research, and continual maintenance to coordinate each setting and bring the whole area to life year 'round.

The Disney landscapes and gardens perform four important functions. First, the landscape enhances the theme of an area, complementing the architecture and other "show" components, setting the stage and helping to "tell the story." For instance, tropical plants add just the right touch to the Jungle Cruise and geometrically pruned shrubs provide futuristic ambiance in Tomorrowland®.

Second, the landscape furnishes a neutral and smooth transition area from one "set" to the next. For example,

in EPCOT®, green grass, trees, and shrubs provide a natural transition from showcase to showcase. These areas create continuity between the "countries," blending all the potentially competing visual elements.

Third, the landscapes act as screens for views and noises from "behind the scenes," discreetly focusing attention elsewhere and minimizing intrusions. Tall stands of trees, thick rows of hedges, and grassy berms conveniently and attractively provide cover to parking lots and service areas.

By far the most important role the landscapes and gardens play is in making the Parks and Resorts exciting places to visit. Vast expanses of colorful flowers, whimsical topiary figures, gorgeous hanging baskets, and all the other landscape "stars" add mystery, drama, adventure, romance, fantasy, and comedy to the Disney landscape stages.

The Landscape Design Process

It's difficult to imagine the Walt Disney Theme Parks and Resorts without all their spectacular landscapes. The trees, flowers, shrubs, and grass all contribute to enjoyment of the experience.

The Disney landscape design approach has always been motivated by a belief that plants play a very important role in making the landscapes the "people spaces" that they are. Therefore, all landscape designs center on concerns for the thousands of Disney guests who visit the Parks and Resorts each day. The people-oriented designs must be functional and provide an enjoyable, comfortable, and entertaining experience for the guests.

Disney landscapes are constantly reviewed, re-planted, revised, and renewed. The process is ongoing and ever-evolving and every landscape project is a team effort, from design and installation to maintenance.

Teamwork, combined with the right mixture of talents and a shared goal, are the common denominators in turning landscape dreams into reality.

Disney Horticultural Philosophies

The Disney horticultural "show" is famous worldwide, but there are five key traditions that have become known as uniquely Disney in their nature. Those elements are "theming," color, instant landscaping, horticultural specialties, and experimentation.

Theming

"Theming" is a word coined by The Walt Disney Company and, horticulturally speaking, it refers to the landscape supporting and enhancing the theme of a particular area. A theme may be realistic or historical, such as the Victorian surroundings of Main Street, U.S.A.® or the Shakespearean cottage garden at United Kingdom in EPCOT. Sometimes a theme is imaginary, like in Future World in EPCOT or Fantasyland® or The Haunted Mansions in Disneyland Park and Magic Kingdom Park®.

Disney gardeners select plants, trees, and shrubs to realistically match a setting or to provide make-believe appeal. When native plants won't provide authenticity or survive in a particular climate, look-alike plants are substituted to create the realism.

Color

One thing Disney guests notice immediately is the blaze of landscape color everywhere they look. They "ooh and ahh" over ornate gardens, admire eye-level hanging baskets draped with flowers, and stop to watch the sun set behind a woodland silhouette. The landscape colors are chosen carefully to artistically coordinate with the surroundings and particular theme of the area, setting the mood for the whole scene.

Disney gardeners are constantly conducting tests and research for more vibrant colors, bigger and longer lasting blooms, and new and improved plant varieties. Their ongoing work results in the horticultural kaleidoscope of color seen year 'round in the Disney landscapes.

Instant Landscaping

Instant landscaping, simply stated, is the installation of mature plants, including trees, shrubs, sod, or blooming flowers, to create the look of a well-established landscape. Large trees can also provide better proportion and scale to an area. For example, tall palms planted near Spaceship Earth in EPCOT befit the massive dimensions of the structure.

Large beds of declining annuals are routinely replaced with new batches of already-blooming flowers for a fresh spot of color. Large shade trees pop up overnight. Acres of turf are unrolled like carpeting for new attractions and resorts.

Horticultural Specialties

Disney horticultural specialties, like topiary figures, hanging baskets, poinsettia trees, cascading or floating mums, bonsai, and seasonal shows add a touch of fun and visual appeal to the landscapes. The Walt Disney Company has spent years testing and perfecting these horticultural techniques.

Experimentation

The Walt Disney Company has become a leader in showcasing innovation in gardening. Horticultural researchers test various plants, products, and techniques to find ways to improve the landscape show. Bedding plants are tested to find those exhibiting the most disease resistance, the best color, and the greatest longevity. Experiments with fertilizers and soils are conducted to ensure that the "show" always looks its best and is constantly improving. This unending experimentation also includes practicing creative horticulture techniques and trying new ideas.

Environmental Commitments

Disney has embraced, encouraged, and practiced a philosophy of environmental protection on a company-wide basis. For example, a large portion of the Walt Disney World Resort property is designated for conservation and open space. A conservation and wildlife sanctuary on this land is the home to a variety of plants and trees, and protects some of Florida's abundant wildlife. A mile-long section of this conservation area can be explored at Fort Wilderness and Discovery Island on the Wilderness Swamp Trail.

Disney participates in many projects encouraging landscape beautification and environmental awareness. Water conservation techniques, such as using recycled water for irrigation, vehicle washing, and in decorative fountains, are also being practiced.

Integrated pest management techniques as an alternative to chemical pesticides are utilized. Review preference is given to products incorporating recycled materials and those that are "environmentally friendly." Earth Day and Arbor Day are celebrated each year, drawing attention to the state of our fragile ecosystem.

Trees are salvaged, saved, or protected through relocation or design modifications. Much of the Disney landscape waste is recycled and used as a soil amendment. Composted sludge produced by the Disney Waste Water Treatment Plant is being used as a top-dressing and a soil amendment throughout Walt Disney World Resort. More natural (versus chemical) fertilizers are being used. White paper, aluminum cans, cardboard, wooden pallets, and plastic nursery pots are recycled.

The Disney Wilderness Preserve, 8,500 acres of land located approximately 12 miles south of Walt Disney World Resort, is another significant area preserved by the Company. The land was donated to the Nature Conservancy with a long-term management program funded by Disney. It preserves the habitats of many threatened and endangered species. Scrub jays, sandhill cranes, woodstorks, and ospreys make the Preserve their home.

These are just a few of the many ways Disney is helping to protect our environment. Further research, environmentally safe horticultural practices, and promoting environmental awareness will continue as Disney grows.

*"If certain events continue,
much of America's natural beauty will
become nothing more than a memory. The
natural beauty of America is a treasure found
nowhere else in the world. Our forests, waters,
grasslands, and wildlife must be wisely
protected and used. I urge all citizens to join
the effort to save America's natural beauty....
It's our America — do something
to preserve its beauty, strength,
and natural wealth."*

Walt Disney

A colorful carpet of flower
spreads out
before Spacesh
Earth in
EPCOT.

Gardening is a personal adventure. It's a hobby enjoyed by literally millions of people around the world. For some gardeners there is a pure joy in watching a seed sprout, grow, and become a full-fledged blooming spectacle before their eyes. Others are often content to just commune with nature and get their hands dirty once in a while. For certain adventurous folks, it's a moving challenge to nurture and cultivate the earth to produce their own food, like modern-day pioneers. Some people find being outdoors in the fresh air, working with the soil and plants is a relaxing experience like no other. Often, dedicated gardeners find one particular plant group they decide to specialize in, like orchids, herbs, irises, roses, or bromeliads. Gardening can be a unifying experience for all involved — bonding with each other and the earth.

A closer look reveals a different world.

A "Green Thumb" Primer

Gardening can sometimes be as frustrating as it is rewarding. It's a series of trial and error, and a battle against pests, the weather, poor soil conditions, and a multitude of other factors each specific to a particular location. You must understand your climate zone, what types of soil you have and what you can do to improve it, what plants tolerate shade or sun, how much you need to water, and what kinds of plants fit into your landscape.

Everyone experiences these problems when gardening — you're not alone. Over the years, Disney horticulturists on both coasts have worked endlessly, experimenting with every gardening aspect from plant types to watering and planting methods, perfecting their craft. Use this philosophy in your own landscape. Practice the basics and you'll have a green thumb. If something doesn't work, act like a detective and try to determine why. Ask yourself if you watered accordingly, fed it regularly, and planted it properly and in an appropriate location. If you're still stumped, ask garden center personnel, consult with an agricultural extension agent, or check a gardening book. You may even have the solution in your home library!

The Science of Gardening

Plant Names and Cultivars

Plant taxonomy is the term for the classification, naming, and identification of plants. All plants are given long name classifications consisting of: Kingdom, Division, Subdivision, Class, Order, Family, Genus, Species, and sometimes Cultivar. When put together, the descriptive names are understood and accepted by plant experts around the world.

For most home gardeners only the last three classifications are of importance and it is those names that typically appear on plant tags. The genus and species are expressed in Latin. The genus can refer to the name of the botanist or explorer who first discovered the plant and named it. The species typically describes the plant or its place of origin.

Transvaal daisy — Gerbera jamesonii

New gardeners sometimes don't realize there is more to a plant name than the common references, such as "daisy" or "geranium." Experienced gardeners recognize the importance of plant cultivar names when making their garden selections. The term **cultivar** is short for "cultivated variety." A cultivar is a plant that has been produced under very controlled circumstances versus a plant that occurs naturally in the wild. If you select the appropriate cultivar for your area, chances are very good that the plant will do well in your landscape.

ranium — Pelargonium hortorum

Botanically Named Disney Plants

Bill Evans, the well-known Disneyland landscape architect, is an avid plantsman. He regularly collected new plants he found during his travels around the world and introduced them into Disney Theme Parks to study their adaptability. One exotic plant he bred is called a *Philodendron evansii* that was fittingly named in his honor.

Swiss Family Treehouse in Magic Kingdom Par

The Swiss Family Treehouse, "growing" in the Magic Kingdom, has been unofficially christened the *Disneydendron eximius* (meaning "out of the ordinary Disney tree"). The steel and concrete tree weighs 200 tons and is covered with 800,000 vinyl leaves. Disneyland boasts a similar tree house, the *Disneydendron semperflorens grandis* or a "large, ever-blooming Disney tree." This tree was "planted" in 1962 and now has such jungle-like foliage coverage that little distinction can be made between the real manzanita branches and the 300,000 vinyl leaves. The manmade tree weighs 150 tons and is anchored by 62 banyan-like concrete "roots" that reach 42 feet into the ground.

Plant Terminology

Annuals vs. Perennials

Some flowers are labeled as **annuals** and others are called **perennials**. The essential difference is that annuals live and grow beautifully for one season up to one year. They produce an abundance of stunning blossoms, then go into decline because they have seeded and finished their life cycle, and need to be removed. Perennials, in comparison, are a more permanent addition to the landscape and have a life span of over two years. Their stems and leaves die back during the cold months, but their roots remain alive. Each spring, the roots generate new and larger plants. A skillfully planned perennial garden will produce a colorful, ever-changing floral

display throughout the growing season. Most longtime gardeners prefer to plant a combination of annuals and perennials for maximum impact.

A few plants are classified as **biennials**. Typically, these plants complete their life cycle over two seasons or two years and then die. In the first year, they grow from seed into leafy plants (which is usually when the home gardener purchases and plants them) and the next year they produce flowers, set seed, and die.

Perennial — Iceland Poppy

Annual — Zinnia

Evergreen vs. Deciduous

Trees are classified as either **evergreen** or **deciduous**. Evergreen trees, as the name implies, do not lose their leaves and usually look the same throughout the year. Deciduous trees shed their leaves each year, exposing interesting branch configurations and bark textures, and produce a spectacular fall foliage show in certain colder regions of the country.

Evergreen Tree

Deciduous Tree

Cold Hardiness

Success in your garden also has much to do with the plants' cold hardiness. For example, it would mean sure death to a cold-sensitive plant to put it in the ground before all chance of frost was over.

Climate maps, like the one shown on page 27, are general guidelines indicating temperature extremes and are typically displayed in numbered zones. These zones are further defined by "last frost date" which is usually the best time to begin planting to avoid damage from cold temperatures. If you select plants best suited to your zone and plant them at the right times, you'll be successful in your garden. Remember, even though you may know your plant zone, there are also "microclimates" within your own landscape that can affect plant growth. These microclimates change with exposure to sunlight, wind, elevation, and other variables.

An easy way to determine if a plant is appropriate for your landscape is to first find your location on the plant hardiness zone map. Then, when you're purchasing plants, look at the plant tag or catalog information to determine if the plants are suitable for your environment. If your zone is indicated, the plant should grow well in your landscape.

USDA Plant Hardiness Zone Map

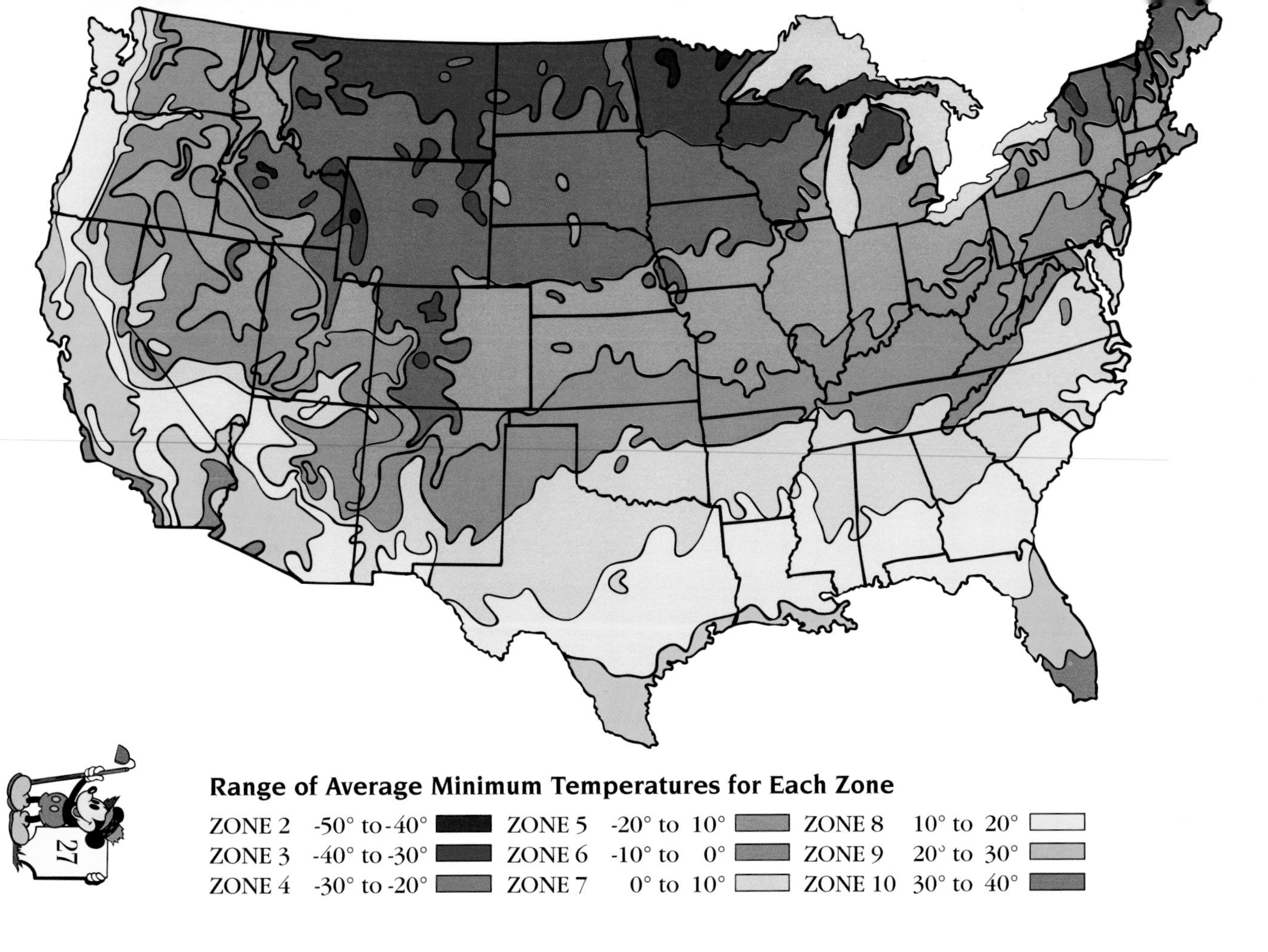

Propagation

Propagation refers to the various ways new plants can be grown from old plants. There are several easy ways to propagate plants including planting seeds, grafting, taking cuttings, air layering, plant division, and tissue culturing.

Seeds

The simplest method used to propagate plants is to sow the seeds directly in the garden, or plant them in nursery flats or in a cold frame. Once sprouted, the young plants are kept evenly moist and fed lightly. After the seedlings have produced their first set of "true leaves," they are thinned out and spaced evenly in their garden location.

Grafting

Grafting is an ancient horticultural art. There are many types, including "budding." This is basically the insertion of a short piece of stem (the *scion*) from the host plant, bearing one or more buds, into the donor plant (the *stock* or *understock*) to form a union that eventually grows together as one plant. If you graft a fruit tree, for example, you can create one tree that bears several varieties of fruit all with different ripening times! There are many ways to graft depending upon what plants you are trying to propagate. Whatever method you use, the cambium layer (between the bark and the wood) of both the scion and the stock must be perfectly aligned when joined and be close botanical relatives for a successful graft. This union is often sealed with grafting tape or wax.

Cuttings

Taking **stem, root, or leaf cuttings** is another simple way to propagate plants. To make **stem cuttings**, 3" to 5" lengths of healthy plant stems are cut just below the tips of recent growth. The leaves are removed from the bottom 1½" of the cuttings and the bottoms (where each cut was made) are dipped into a rooting powder. The stems are gently pushed about an inch into a flat of moistened media, such as vermiculite, so they can root. The whole flat is carefully covered with plastic wrap and put in an area of bright, but not direct, sunlight. The plastic is lifted once a day to prevent mold and to circulate the air. When the stems are firmly rooted, they are transplanted into containers or into the garden. Stem cuttings work well with begonia, chrysanthemum, geranium, azalea, bougainvillea, hibiscus, pyracantha, and wisteria, to name a few.

Root cuttings are usually taken in early spring before plants begin their active growth period or in late summer at the end of the growth period. The thickest roots are the best to use and are exposed by gently digging in a section of the root area. Then 1" to 3" pieces are cut and planted horizontally in separate pots of soil or directly into the garden and covered with ½" to 1" of soil. Raspberry, blackberry, plumbago, and Oriental poppy are among the plants you can propagate by taking root cuttings.

Leaf cuttings are made by carefully clipping a leaf stem to 1" or 2". The stem is then gently placed in a moist potting mix and kept at a constant temperature in the shade until the new plant forms. Rex begonia, African violet, and gloxinia respond well to leaf cutting propagation.

Air Layering

Air layering is a good way to increase your supply of shrubs, trees, and larger house plants. A branch ranging in size from the diameter of a pencil to approximately 1" is selected for air layering. A slanting cut is made about one-third of the way through the branch just below a leaf node. A wooden matchstick is inserted sideways in the cut area to keep the cut portion exposed. The cut area is then wrapped generously in damp sphagnum moss and completely covered with plastic and tied securely. After several months, if the layering is successful, roots will appear in the sphagnum moss and the newly rooted plant can be removed from the original plant and planted.

Division

Most perennial plants can be quickly propagated by division. Division is also performed to rejuvenate certain plants and to control plant size. An overcast day is a preferable time to perform the division to avoid excessive root drying from sun and wind exposure. The entire plant is carefully dug up, roots and all. Then the soil is gently hosed or shaken from the root system to expose the "crowns" or growth points of the plants. The plant is divided into clumps that each have a good portion of roots, a section of stem, and a crown with leaves, and then replanted separately. Some plants are easily divided by simply pulling the main clump apart, but others with tough crown areas will require division with a sharp knife.

Tissue Culturing

Tissue culturing is an amazing technique of cloning many plants from one small plant cutting. Scientific research indicates that every living cell in the roots, stems, and leaves of plants contains enough genetic information to produce a new plant if placed in the proper (and very sterile) growing conditions.

The prepared plant tissue is set in agar (a solidified nutrient liquid) in a test tube. This liquid contains nutrient salts, sugars, vitamins, and growth regulators. The plant begins to grow, and in a few months, it's possible to propagate several thousand plants from a single plant cell! Banana, pineapple, orchid, and ginger are among the plants that can be propagated through tissue culturing procedures.

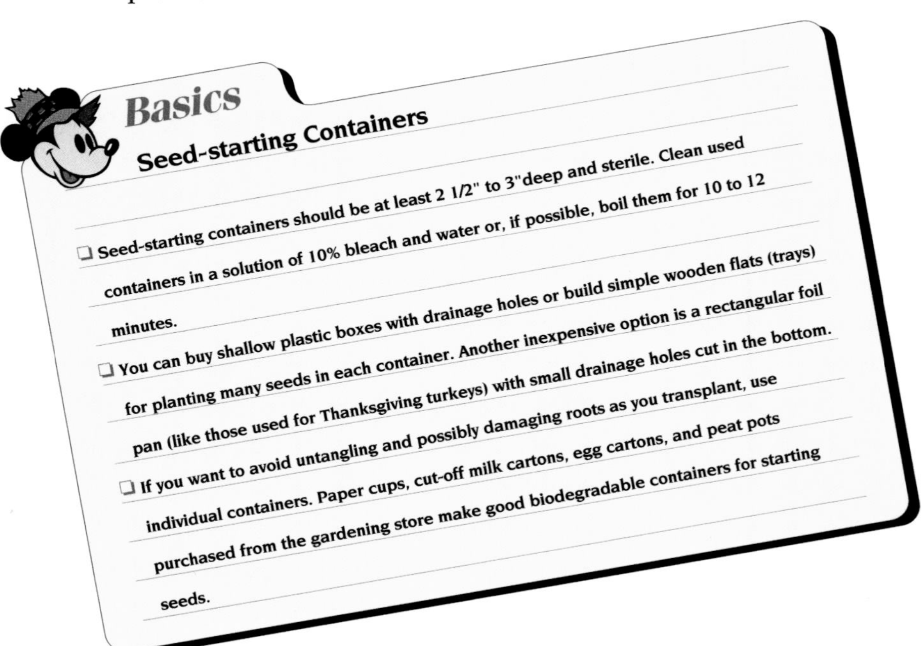

Basics

Seed-starting Containers

- Seed-starting containers should be at least 2 1/2" to 3"deep and sterile. Clean used containers in a solution of 10% bleach and water or, if possible, boil them for 10 to 12 minutes.
- You can buy shallow plastic boxes with drainage holes or build simple wooden flats (trays) for planting many seeds in each container. Another inexpensive option is a rectangular foil pan (like those used for Thanksgiving turkeys) with small drainage holes cut in the bottom.
- If you want to avoid untangling and possibly damaging roots as you transplant, use individual containers. Paper cups, cut-off milk cartons, egg cartons, and peat pots purchased from the gardening store make good biodegradable containers for starting seeds.

How to Start Your Own Seeds

What You'll Need

- ❑ A packet of seeds
- ❑ A 2-quart bag of potting soil
- ❑ Seed-starting container with drainage holes
- ❑ Gravel, coarse sand, or sphagnum moss for drainage
- ❑ Bottle mister
- ❑ Plastic wrap

1. Put a thin layer of clean gravel, coarse sand, or sphagnum moss inside on the bottom of your seed-starting container. Fill the container with moistened potting soil to within ½" of the rim, pressing gently to level.

2. Bury large and medium-sized seeds at a depth of two to three times their diameter, 1" apart. Medium-sized seeds are planted at ½" apart. Fine seeds simply need to be pressed into the surface and dusted over with a thin layer of sand or potting soil. Check the back of the seed packet for sowing instructions because some seeds require light to germinate and only need to be sprinkled across the top of the soil.

(Continued ...)

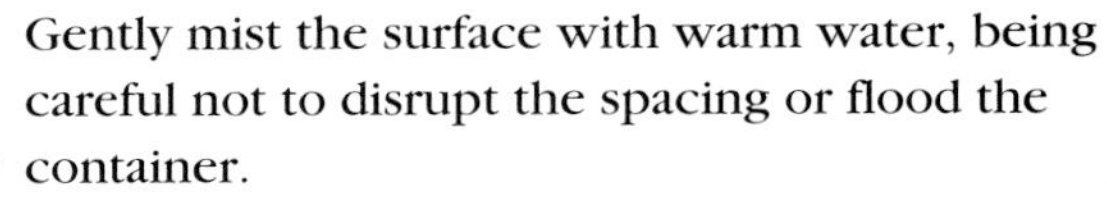

Gently mist the surface with warm water, being careful not to disrupt the spacing or flood the container.

Cover with plastic wrap to maintain a high moisture level so the seeds don't dry out. Don't allow the plastic to touch the soil and make some small slits in the plastic for air flow.

Put the container in a warm spot that stays above 65° F, keeping the soil moist, but not soggy. If mold appears, your drainage is probably not adequate or you may be watering too much. Remove the plastic covering and extract the moldy seeds. Add more holes to the plastic to keep the mold in check and recover.

Remove the plastic as soon as you see green leav emerging. Maintain a temperature of about 70° F and mist daily with warm water. If the seedlings begin to stretch toward a light source, move the to a sunnier or brighter location.

7 When the plants are 2" or taller and have developed their first set of leaves, weed out the less hardy seedlings. Water less frequently now and let the soil surface dry out between soakings, but continue using warm water only. Seedlings benefit from as much full sunlight a day as possible. Move the plants to a sunnier window or outside if necessary.

8 Before placing the plants in the garden, it is advisable to transplant them into containers with fresh potting soil so they develop stronger roots. If you originally planted the seeds in small pots, select pots one size larger for transplanting. If you planted the seeds in flats, transplant into 4" pots. Expect them to go into "shock," but don't worry, they'll perk back up.

9 Two weeks before transferring seedlings to the garden, "harden them off" by watering less frequently. In cold climates, put the containers outside in a shady, protected area for an hour or two during the warmest part of the day to get them accustomed to being outside. Increase the exposure over 10 days until they are able to stay out all day, but bring them in at night to avoid frost damage. When all chance of frost is over, plant 'em!

Ingredients for Plant Growth

Soil Basics

What is Soil?

Soil is a combination of mineral particles, organic matter, air, and water. But not all soils are created equal. Sometimes you have to correct or amend a soil with manure, sand, peat moss, or other organic matter, for example, to ensure good plant growth. Compost, partially decomposed sawdust, wood chips, and milled pine bark also provide nutrients to soil organisms, which in turn, help convert insoluble soil nutrients into available plant nutrients.

Soil texture refers to the size of the soil particles and available space for water, roots, and air to travel through the soil. The best soils are a balanced combination of silt, sand, and clay.

The arrangement of individual soil particles into groups in the soil is termed **soil structure.** The most desirable soil structure is one that is granular since air and water can move easily among the soil particles contributing to plant vigor.

Moisture retention is the ability of the soil to hold water in the pore spaces and correlates to the amount of space between soil particles. Moisture retention, like nutrient retention, is vastly improved with the addition of organic matter.

Soil depth is important to the management of plant growth. In general, deeply prepared soils have increased water-holding and nutrient storage abilities.

Soil sterilization with steam is done to soil contaminated with disease organisms, insects, weeds, or other pests. Homeowners can accomplish this by covering the soil with clear plastic for a month in the heat of the summer.

Poor drainage causes the soil particles to be always saturated with water preventing air from getting to the plant roots and leading to possible plant death. This trouble can be eliminated by increasing the soil's aeration by digging down and breaking up firm layers of soil, building up the bed by adding sand or pea gravel, or by installing drainage systems to carry away excess water.

Soil types include clay, sand, muck or peat, and loam. Before you plant, it's a good idea to determine your soil type. Soil sampling and testing allows you to determine exactly what fertilizers or amendments are needed since soils constantly undergo change. You can use do-it-yourself pH and soil testing kits, have a commercial laboratory test for you, or enlist the help of garden center personnel or an agricultural extension agent. Follow their recommendations before you begin a project and you'll have better success.

What is pH?

The term "pH" refers to the acidity or alkalinity of a soil. The pH of a soil affects plant growth in many ways: it affects the root system's ability to absorb water and nutrients; it has an effect on soil microorganisms and the availability of essential nutrients; and affects the magnitude to which toxic substances enter through plant roots.

The pH scale ranges from 1.0 (very acidic) to 14.0 (very alkaline), with 7.0 being neutral. Most garden plants grow best when the pH is between 5.5 and 6.5.

Do-it-yourself pH Testing

If you plan to test soil pH yourself, the samples and test equipment should be at room temperature for the most accurate results. When using a probe unit, immerse the probe to the top of the sample cup holder. Don't dunk the entire probe unit into the sample because the top isn't usually waterproofed. The moisture could penetrate the unit and short circuit the probe's elements.

You can avoid cross-contamination by rinsing just the probe with distilled water between sample readings. Also, avoid forcing the probe into hard earth by softening the soil with water in the spot to be tested and remove grass, pebbles, and other debris.

Be sure to avoid using test equipment near magnetic objects because they can alter readings. It's very important to keep the metal plates on test equipment clean. Fingerprints or oily marks can reduce the flow of current and give you inaccurate readings. You can clean pH testers with a soft, lint-free rag or paper towel, when necessary.

How to Prepare the Soil Bed

What You'll Need

- ❑ Soil pH test kit
- ❑ A good soil mix of peat moss, coarse sand, composted pine bark, and wood chips
- ❑ Cultivator or rototiller
- ❑ Garden rake
- ❑ High nitrogen granular fertilizer with micronutrients

1 Evaluate the pH of the soil. A pH of 5.5 to 6.5 is desirable. Add amendments to bring the pH to the proper level.

2 Remove all plant debris, such as root balls, dead leaves, twigs, and weeds, with the garden rake.

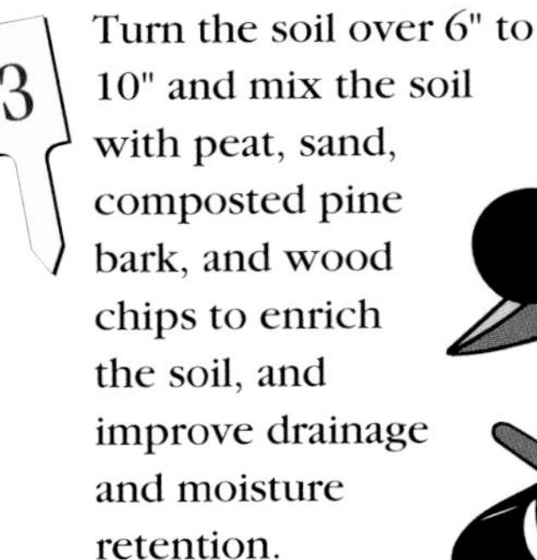

3 Turn the soil over 6" to 10" and mix the soil with peat, sand, composted pine bark, and wood chips to enrich the soil, and improve drainage and moisture retention.

4 Spread the granular fertilizer on the soil and till with the cultivat or rototiller.

5 Smooth the bed with the garden rake to the desired level. Now you're ready to plant!

Basics

How to Prepare Your Own Soil Mix

What You'll Need

- ❑ Compost ❑ Peat moss ❑ Coarse sand ❑ Decomposed pine bark ❑ Wood chips
- ❑ Plastic or steel tub for mixing ❑ Garden hoe for mixing

The above soil mix has provided satisfactory results for Disney gardeners in Florida. Combine four parts compost, two parts peat moss, two parts coarse sand, one part decomposed pine bark, and one part wood chips. This is a rich soil mix with good moisture retention qualities. The sand keeps the soil loose and promotes adequate drainage. The compost, pine bark, and wood chips help to develop beneficial microbial activity

Soil Problems

Common soil problems include acidity, alkalinity, nutrient deficiency, salinity, and shallow, compacted soil. Each one of these problems (except for really compacted soil) is easy for the home gardener to remedy.

Acidity

Acidity typically occurs where there is heavy rainfall, in soil with a high amount of organic material, and is usually associated with sandy soil. Some plants prefer more acid soils (like azalea, rhododendron, and camellia), but many plants thrive in a more alkaline soil. Add lime, calcium, magnesium, bone meal, pulverized egg shells, clam shells, oyster shells, or wood ashes (also discourages bugs) to take care of the problem of high acidity. Avoid hydrated lime because it's caustic and may burn seeds or young transplants.

Azaleas

Alkalinity

Alkalinity is common in areas where rainfall is light and where gardeners water with softened water. Alkaline soil is usually high in calcium carbonate (lime) and several other minerals. Gypsum, iron, ammonium sulfate, sulfur, sawdust, wood chips, leaf mold, peat moss, or pine needles help neutralize alkaline soils, but in extreme cases it is best to plant in improved soil, rich in compost, peat, or manure, in raised beds or containers.

Chlorosis

Chlorosis is a condition where plants are unable to efficiently take iron from the soil up into their root systems. Leaf yellowing is a common indicator. You can correct chlorosis by applying chelated iron or iron sulfate or by spraying foliage with a liquid iron solution.

Nutrient Deficiency

Nutrient deficiency (especially the big three — nitrogen, phosphorus, and potassium) can be easily corrected with application of either chemical or organic fertilizers. Nutrient deficiency can be recognized by slow or stunted growth, absence or lack of flowers, straggly looking plants, and discolored leaves.

When you buy a "complete" fertilizer it is usually marked with a series of three numbers, such as 5-10-5. These numbers indicate the percentages of nitrogen, phosphorus, and potassium — in that order — contained in the package. **Nitrogen** promotes rapid growth of green leaves and stems, in particular. **Phosphorus** regulates a plant's growth, encourages early root formation, and assists in nutrient uptake by the roots. It also is important in promoting flower and seed production. **Potassium** plays a role in disease resistance and production of the plant's sugar, starch, and cellulose, contributing to the plant tissue strength.

If a plant is deficient in nitrogen, typically there is a yellowing of the entire plant, especially in the lower leaves which tend to drop. If a plant doesn't seem to be growing, perhaps it's deficient in phosphorus. If your plant doesn't have a strong enough stem to hold the leaves and blossoms, try additional potassium.

There are other signs of nutrient deficiencies, too. A need for additional magnesium could be indicated by a yellowing on the margins and centers of older leaves or by leaf drop. Try adding iron when you notice pronounced yellowing of newer leaves (you'll see veins appearing as fine green lines), or dwarfed or reduced growth. A deficiency in manganese may be the problem if you spot mottled yellowing of the leaf between the main leaf veins or if the leaves change to red or purple.

Salinity

Salinity, an excess build-up of salt in the soil, is a common problem in arid and semiarid terrains. It can cause alkalinity, prevent germination, stunt growth, burn foliage, and kill plants. It is also caused by frequent, shallow watering, especially with softened water, and certain fertilizers. If there is no compacted soil, periodic slow and deep watering can help wash the salts beyond the roots. You can also work elemental sulfur, compost, mulch, or leaf mold into the soil to help solve the problem.

Compacted Soil

Shallow, compacted soil, also known as "hardpan," can prevent roots and water from penetrating the soil. If, when you water, it doesn't filter into your dry soil after 30 minutes, you probably have compacted soil. Sometimes this compaction is a natural phenomenon and other times it's a manmade problem. This is a fairly troublesome soil to work with and some people go to the extreme measure of bringing in a backhoe and plowing the soil to a depth of several feet. Others go to the expense of having a landscape architect design a drainage system or drain tiles.

Try raised bed gardening if you have compacted soil.

If you're really determined to try your hand at gardening in compacted soil, rent a rototiller and till the soil from 12" to 24". Then add amendments like oak leaf mulch, rice hulls, naturalized redwood, or gypsum to make the soil less likely to compact. Don't forget to incorporate some slow-release fertilizer, too. Eventually, these amendments will break down and your soil will become compacted again. You may have to re-till every three to four years. If the compacted soil is in an area that receives any kind of "traffic," like lawns, you may want to aerate the area every year or so with a soil aerator. The most practical, least expensive, and most successful way to garden if you have severely compacted soil is to try raised beds or container gardening.

Fertilizer Basics

You must fertilize your plants, flowers, and lawns to keep them happy and healthy. Think of fertilizers as daily nutrition, not as a medicine to be used when something is wrong. It's best to stay on a schedule with fertilizing rather than letting the plants and grass tell you they're hungry with slow growth and yellowing leaves.

Types

There are several different types of fertilizers, including complete, special purpose, slow-release, and organic. Complete fertilizer contains the three primary nutritional elements (nitrogen, phosphorus, and potassium) at varying rates and comes in either dry or liquid form. Most gardeners prefer this type because of the convenience, however, you can buy the major nutrients separately.

Dry fertilizer comes in granular, powder, or pellet form and is scattered on the ground, worked into the soil, or buried deep in the root zone and dissolves over time.

Liquid fertilizers are popular among gardeners who raise annuals and perennials in containers because the plant nutrients become available to the leaves and roots immediately. Liquid fertilizer contains soluble granules that are mixed with water and can be applied to the leaves or surrounding soil during a regular watering. Liquid fertilizers are also useful where drip-irrigation is used.

Special purpose fertilizers are formulated with specific nutrient contents for particular plants, like roses, azaleas, citrus, or orchids.

Slow-release fertilizers are dry or plastic-encased granular fertilizers that last from three to 14 months and release their nutrients over time as you water, eliminating the need for more frequent fertilizing. The most important benefit here is the slow and steady release of nitrogen. Nitrogen is the most-needed nutrient and one which is leached from the soil very rapidly.

Natural organic fertilizers are created from materials derived from a plant or animal, such as manure, bone meal, or fish emulsion. Organic fertilizers are generally low in nutrient content and are relatively slow release because bacterial action is required to release the nutrients.

Application

Read the label carefully, twice if necessary, and apply according to the directions. Follow all stated precautions. Solid fertilizer can be applied by hand, a gravity feed spreader, or rotary spreader. Liquid fertilizers are easily applied by attaching your hose to a spray applicator.

Mulching

Mulching is basically a soil cover and is important for many reasons: (1) it efficiently controls long-term weed growth better and more safely than any herbicides; (2) during dry conditions and drought, mulching helps plants survive by aiding in moisture retention; (3) it insulates against harsh winter temperatures where the mercury drops below freezing for at least part of the year, and prevents the ground from heaving; (4) certain mulches can enhance the appearance of your landscape; and (5) organic mulch improves the soil as it decomposes.

Mulch sources include bark, mixed tree trimmings, sawdust, pine needles, pine boughs, straw, grass clippings, leaves, stone, and a variety of other materials. Many commercially available mulches are reasonably priced and very attractive.

Pine needles

Bark

When mulching your garden, be sure to weed and water before you spread the mulch. Watering first ensures the dry mulch won't rob the soil and plants of moisture. Avoid rot and rodent damage by pulling the mulch away from plant stems and tree trunks.

Stone

Composting

Compost is a soft, crumbly, brown or black material resulting from the decomposition of organic matter over time. Its value as an organic soil amendment is much greater than its worth as a nutrient source, but composting is an environmentally wise choice and will improve your garden soil.

The easiest, but least efficient, method of composting is to pile up grass clippings, leaves, other garden materials, and vegetable waste from the kitchen and wait for them to decompose. In six weeks to six months, depending upon temperature, rainfall, and size of the material, the compost will be ready for the garden.

A better method for most gardeners is to stack the material four to six feet high inside a slatted bin or mesh wire enclosure. Aerate the material at least once a week by turning it with a pitchfork or shovel and moisten the pile as needed to keep it about as wet as a wrung-out sponge. To speed the decomposition, add a few handfuls of lime once a week.

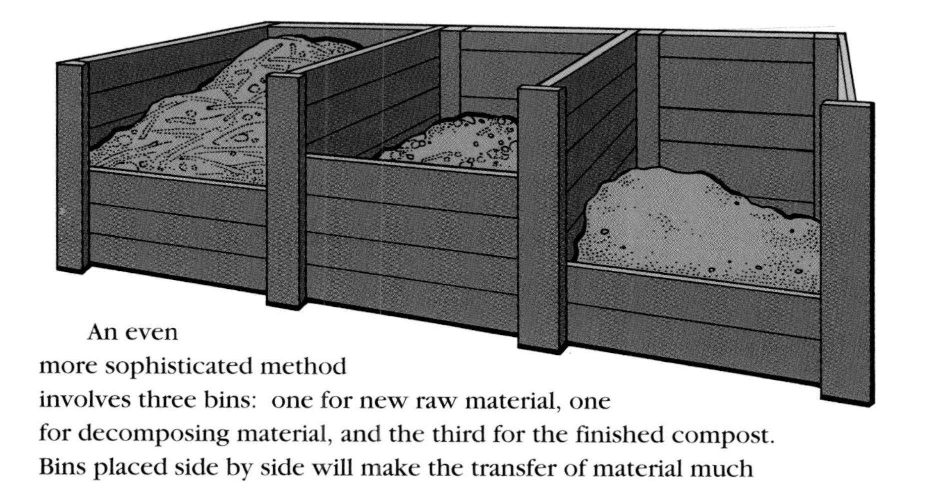

An even more sophisticated method involves three bins: one for new raw material, one for decomposing material, and the third for the finished compost. Bins placed side by side will make the transfer of material much simpler.

Locating the pile in full sun also hastens the process, but you should protect the pile from excessive and drying winds. Another pointer is to chop the materials as finely as possible before you add them to the pile. Certain materials can be "mowed" by the lawnmower before their addition to the pile.

Watering Basics

Just like human beings, plants need water to survive. Some plants, like grasses and trees, send their roots deep into the ground where they get the majority of their needed moisture. However, most garden plants, especially flowers, need some additional water for healthy growth. Establish a watering schedule and stick to it. It's not a good idea to wait until your plants tell you they're thirsty with their dull, rolling, wilting, and dropping leaves.

There are many variables when it comes to how much water is the right amount of water: soil and plant type, temperature, humidity, season, light intensity, wind, and location. You'll learn what kind of watering your garden requires by observing your plants and following the basic principles of watering.

Water penetrates the soil based on the soil's composition. Water seeps through sandy soil deeply and quickly and needs much more frequent watering than clay soil, which holds about three times as much water as sandy soil. It's best to water clay soil with a sprinkler because it distributes water evenly and slowly. It's preferable to use the "on-off" method — 10 minutes on, 20 minutes off, 10 minutes on, 20 minutes off, until the ground is saturated. Follow the same rules for sloped terrain to avoid runoff. Clay soils need a drying-out period between waterings to allow air back into the soil, too. Unlike other soil types, if you have a thin layer of topsoil over hardpan, water lightly and frequently.

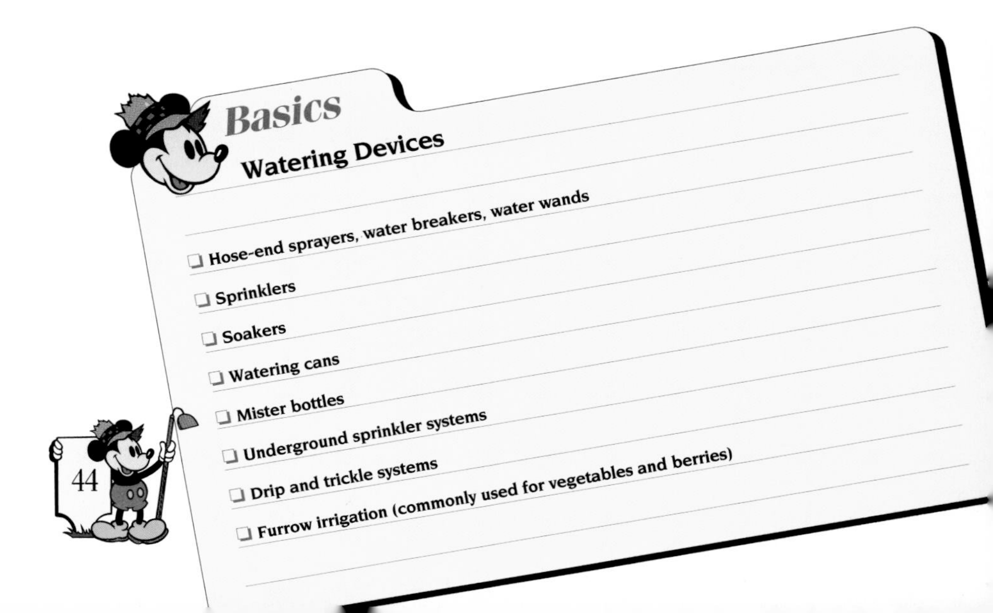

One of the keys to watering properly is to water well and observe how long it takes for the soil to dry out. If you water too much and too often there is a good chance you'll damage or even kill the root systems by depleting the air necessary for proper growth. If you water too lightly and infrequently, you'll end up with shallow-rooted plants that are more prone to dying off during times of drought or high temperatures.

The best time to water is early in the morning because you get less evaporation and reduce the chance of invasion by disease-causing organisms. Plants stay damp throughout the night and if they are watered early in the morning, they have all day to dry out. Watering in the middle of the day can cause leaf burn because the water acts like a magnifying glass when the noontime sun hits the leaves.

Watering Container Plants

Container-grown plants offer a special watering challenge. They tend to dry out quickly, sometimes requiring several waterings a day! You can determine when a container plant needs water by poking your finger into the soil. If the top inch of soil feels dry, it's time to water. Water until you see water running out of the drainage holes. If your container has a saucer, dump the water out of the saucer once the water stops flowing from the holes so the plant doesn't end up with root rot. This frequent watering depletes fertilizers quickly, so fertilize your container plants often.

Watering Tips

- ❑ Don't turn hoses on full blast. Use a water breaker or soaker to soften the stream of water.
- ❑ Bedding plants should always be watered before planting. Once planted, the plants should be watered in well for good plant establishment and to help eliminate air pockets.
- ❑ Watering early in the day is best, but if you can't, wait until before dusk, avoiding the heat of day.
- ❑ Newly planted trees and shrubs should be planted with a raised ring of soil made just inside the "drip line" around them. Water in three times, then the ring may be leveled and mulched over.
- ❑ Remember to turn the automatic irrigation clock back on if you turned it off before planting.
- ❑ Water thoroughly to encourage deep roots. Shallow watering may produce only surface root growth.
- ❑ Treat moisture-loving plants to a "fog shower" using a fog nozzle to increase humidity in the vicinity of these plants.
- ❑ Keep the end of the hose off the ground to avoid contamination from soil-borne disease microbes.
- ❑ Try not to use softened water because it creates a salt build-up on the soil.
- ❑ Water on cooler days in summer and avoid windy days to avoid excessive evaporation.
- ❑ If you use recycled water, which can create an alkaline soil condition, be sure to add gypsum to the soil.
- ❑ Keep sprinkler heads free of clogging debris to ensure even watering.
- ❑ Don't waste water by sprinkling driveways and sidewalks.

Xeriscaping

Cactus and certain euphorbia require little water and can grow in many parts of the country.

Xeriscaping is a water conservation method that is gaining popularity throughout the country, especially in areas of low rainfall and where there are water restrictions. Disney gardeners utilize xeriscaping methods whenever possible.

Xeriscaping basics include: (1) planning and designing the landscape carefully; (2) creating limited areas of lawn; (3) replacing water-loving plants and groundcovers with low water-use plant types; (4) mulching to prevent water evaporation and minimize erosion; (5) improving soil for better water penetration and holding capacity; (6) employing efficient irrigation methods, like drip systems and timers and watering with recycled ("gray") or reclaimed water, if available; and (7) implementing sound maintenance practices.

Sunlight Basics

The sun is the ultimate source of all energy on earth. Think about that for a moment. Amazing, isn't it? It's true. The sun is responsible for keeping what would be a lifeless world alive and thriving — through its heat and light. The heat, or short-wave radiation as scientists refer to it, makes water evaporate and when it condenses it falls back to earth as nourishing rain. Green plants convert the sun's light (solar energy) into food through a process known as "photosynthesis." Very simply, chlorophyll (the green pigment of plants) traps sunlight in plant leaves, water is drawn up from the plant roots, carbon dioxide is taken from the atmosphere, and through the magic of nature, this combination creates energizing sugar which is stored in the plant leaves and releases life-sustaining oxygen into the air.

What does all this mean for the home gardener? The key point to understand here is that all plants differ in the quality and quantity of sunlight they need (and can tolerate) throughout a day to efficiently store energy and grow properly.

For example, if you plant a shade-loving flower in a spot where it receives sun all day long, what do you suppose will happen? Leaves will become scorched, the plant will droop, probably lose its beautiful buds, and turn into an unrecognizable brown thing.

In comparison, if you place a light-demanding plant in a shady corner it will quickly distort itself as it stretches and reaches for the light it desperately needs to grow. Often, a flowering plant will drop its blooms and expend its energy growing more sun-catching leaves.

Even though the angle of the sun varies dramatically throughout the year, the sun's rays are always the most intense and direct during midday. As a result, south- and west-facing slopes are always warmer and drier because they absorb more of the sun's radiant energy than north- and east-facing slopes. In the northern hemisphere, a north-facing wall receives limited direct sunlight and therefore is much cooler and the area retains more moisture. Also, during midsummer, the sun rises in the northeast and sets in the northwest because of the earth's southern tilt. This means that shade-loving plants located in a northeast or northwest location may burn easily from too much sun exposure during this time of year if they are not watered frequently.

Sunlight dapples the flowers at Disney's Grand Floridian Beach Resort.

On a sunny day during your particular growing seasons, observe your own yard in the early morning, during midday, and in the late afternoon. Make notes about which areas of the yard were receiving sun and which areas were relatively shady. Take these notes with you when making your plant selections.

Here's a pointer savvy gardeners always follow: when you buy your plants READ THE TAG! Most nurseries stick little plastic signs into the soil or loop a plastic information tag around one of the branches. All kinds of great facts can be found on these tags. These little "guides" usually mention what kind of light and water a plant needs, what color any blooms might be, the height it will be at maturity (especially important when you buy a tree), and other information you will need to know when making your plant selections.

Common Plants for Shade

Ageratum
Astilbe
Azalea
Balsam

Begonia
Bergenia
Bleeding Heart
Browallia
Caladium
Camellia
Campanula
Canada Hemlock
Cineraria
Coleus
Columbine
David Viburnum
Daylily
Digitalis
Fern
Flowering Dogwood
Forget-me-nots
Foxglove
Heavenly Bamboo
Heliotrope
Hosta
Impatiens
Jacob's Ladder
Japanese Maple
Kafir Lily
Lady's Mantle
Lily-of-the-Valley
Lobelia
Lungwort
Mignonette
Mondo Grass
Monkey Flower
Mountain Laurel
Nicotiana
Nierembergia
Pansy
Periwinkle
Primrose
Rhododendron

Sweet Alyssum
Trillium
Violet
Virginia Creeper
Wishbone Flower
Yew

Common Sun-tolerant Plants

Aster
Balsam
Bells of Ireland

Calendula
California Poppy
Candytuft
Carnation

Celosia
Chrysanthemum
Clematis
Cleome
Coreopsis
Cosmos
Crape Myrtle
Dahlberg Daisy
Dahlia
Delphinium
Dianthus
Dusty Miller

Euphorbia
Flowering Cabbage
Four-o'clock
Gaillardia
Gazania
Geranium
Goldenrod
Gomphrena
Helianthus
Hollyhock
Larkspur
Liatris
Lunaria
Lupine
Marigold
Morning Glory
Nasturtium
Nicotiana
Nierembergia
Pansy
Penstemon
Peonies
Petunia
Phlox
Poppy
Rudebeckia
Salvia

Sedum
Statice
Sunflower

Viola
Yucca
Zinnia

Tools and Equipment

What You'll Need

You don't need a hardware store full of tools to successfully maintain your landscape, but you do need the right ones. The appropriate tools can save you time, energy, and back strain. Think about your current gardening needs or new plans, check out what's already in your garage, and select from the list of basic tools. Remember, many of the larger tools and equipment can be rented from local stores.

For Your Safety

- ❑ Gloves
- ❑ Eye protectors
- ❑ Knee pads (for weeding and planting)
- ❑ Ear plugs (for noisy equipment)

Small Hand Tools

- ❑ Trowel
- ❑ Hand clippers
- ❑ Pruning shears
- ❑ Small pruning saw
- ❑ Hand-held claw cultivator/fork (for close-up work while kneeling or sitting)

Big Hand Tools

- ❑ Long-handled, rounded-point shove (for digging and scooping
- ❑ Long-handled, square-end shovel (for edging and shoveling soil)
- ❑ Potato fork (for cultivating an turning compost)
- ❑ Hoe (for cutting weeds and thick roots and choppin through hard soil)
- ❑ Ax
- ❑ Metal bow rake (for leveling soil and gravel and making seed furrows)
- ❑ Lawn rake (for raking leaves and clippings)
- ❑ Long-handled cultivating hook

Watering

- ❑ Hose
- ❑ Water breaker
- ❑ Watering can
- ❑ Sprinkler
- ❑ Mister
- ❑ Cut-off valve

The Handy Stuff

- ❑ Electric or gas-powered trimmer
- ❑ Electric or gas-powered edger
- ❑ Hand-held sprayer
- ❑ Fertilizer/seed spreader
- ❑ String weed trimmer
- ❑ Liquid fertilizer applicator
- ❑ Wheelbarrow/ garden cart

The Big Stuff

- ❑ Lawnmower
- ❑ Blower
- ❑ Chain saw
- ❑ Sod cutter
- ❑ Rototiller

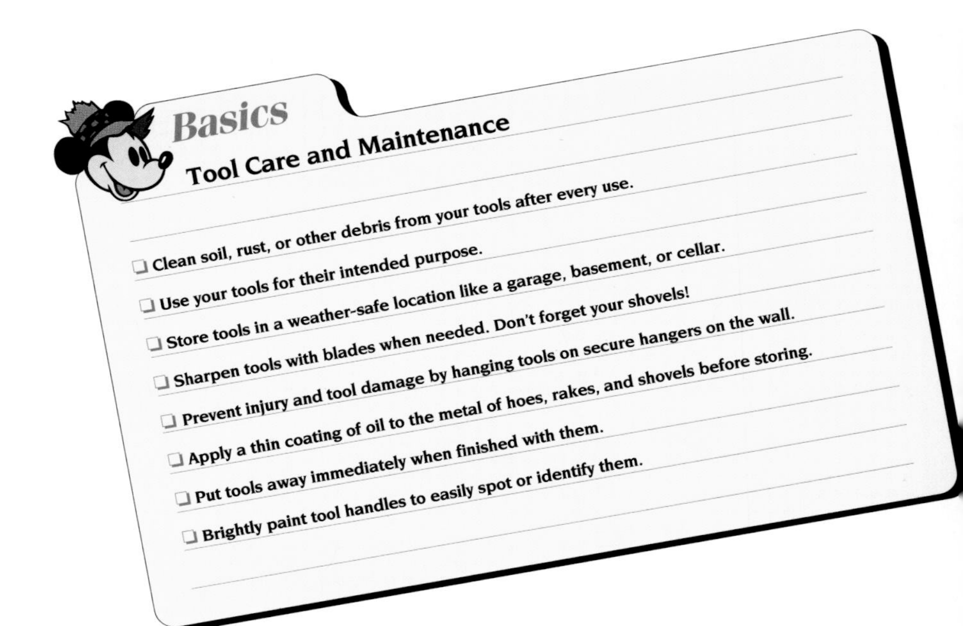

Planting and Transplanting

Planting and transplanting methods vary based upon whether you're planting flowers, trees, shrubs, grass, or vegetables. When you buy plants at the nursery they are typically offered in the following forms: seeds, bulbs, flats, cell packs, very small to tree-sized plastic or metal containers, fiber pots, bare-root, or balled and burlapped.

Follow-up Care

Newly planted or transplanted plants need good follow-up care until they are well established. Water every day for one week. Check soil moisture every day for the first week to a month, depending upon the plant, and water as necessary. Newly planted trees may also require supplemental overhead misting to help them along.

General Guidelines

- ❑ Planting depth recommendations for each plant type should be observed to ensure success. Disney gardeners position plants with a new soil level that is the same or slightly higher than the plant's original soil level to allow for settling. Water collects around trunks and stems and may cause plant disease and eventually death if the top of the root ball is planted below the level of the surrounding soil.
- ❑ Root-pruning is recommended to encourage new growth for pot-bound plants. If roots are matted at the bottom of the pot, circling around the root ball, or actually growing out of the container, it's time for root-pruning. Remove the plant from the pot, unwind and cut off or straighten the large roots encircling the root ball and vertically score the root ball with a sharp knife before transplanting.
- ❑ When planting or transplanting trees and shrubs, use the soil from the planting hole to fill in around the roots and work in gently so the roots are not compressed into a tight mass. If you're adding a granular fertilizer, spread it evenly on the backfill before returning it to the planting hole. When 3" or 4" of soil have been added to the hole around the root ball, firm the soil with your foot to get rid of air pockets. Be careful to avoid the root ball. Continue this process until the hole is filled.
- ❑ Disney landscapers often use slow-release fertilizers in tablet or briquette form when planting and transplanting trees and shrubs. After three-quarters of the soil has been added, the tablets or briquettes are placed in the hole 3" away from the root ball in the recommended number around the plant.

Pest Management

Common Pests

Some of the most well-known pests are creatures who wreak havoc on a yard. They chew their way through your plants in no time, turning your yard into a battleground. Not all critters are bad, though. In fact, some are garden-friendly. Bumble bees, butterflies, worms, and ladybugs are examples of good critters. Remember, some good critters eat some bad pests.

Longtail Mealybug
(Pseudococcus adonid

Natural Organic Controls

Natural organic methods of pest control are the safest. A well-cultivated and fed garden is less likely to have as many problems as one that is not. Raking up yard debris often helps, as does occasionally washing off foliage thoroughly. Also, certain plants, like rhododendron, magnolia, and daylily, are less prone to pest invasion. You can also plant cosmos, daisy, dill, fennel, marigold, nasturtium, and zinnia to attract and feed beneficial insects. Birds can eat an incredible amount of bugs on any given day and you can easily lure them to your yard with bird feeders, ornamental plants with berries, or by planting trees for them to perch in. Snakes, lizards, and frogs can take care of many pests for you!

Beet Leafhopper
(Circulifer tenellus)

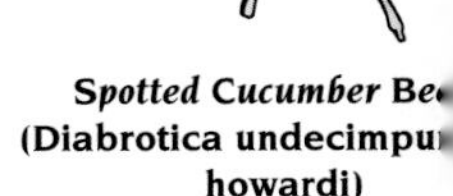

Spotted Cucumber Be
(Diabrotica undecimpu howardi)

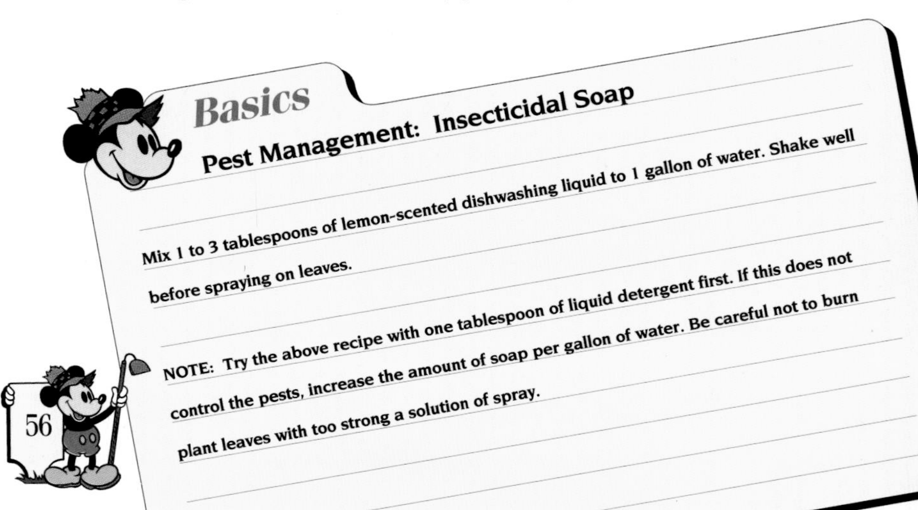

Basics

Pest Management: Insecticidal Soap

Mix 1 to 3 tablespoons of lemon-scented dishwashing liquid to 1 gallon of water. Shake well before spraying on leaves.

NOTE: Try the above recipe with one tablespoon of liquid detergent first. If this does not control the pests, increase the amount of soap per gallon of water. Be careful not to burn plant leaves with too strong a solution of spray.

Basics

Pest Management: Insecticidal Oil

Mix 1 to 3 tablespoons of a refined vegetable oil to 1 gallon of water (Disney gardeners use peanut oil). Spray early in the day and shake well before spraying on leaves.

NOTE: Use a combination of the insecticidal soap and oil sprays at a low concentration at first to see if you get improved results. Gradually increase the oil content, but be aware again of the risk of using too strong a solution so as not to burn the plant leaves.

Basics

Pest Management: Insecticidal Rhubarb Spray

Cut up 1 pound of rhubarb leaves and boil them in 1 quart of water for 1 minute. Strain the mixture through a sieve and add a little bit of nondetergent soap to help the liquid stick to plant leaves when spraying.

NOTE: The active ingredient in rhubarb is oxalic acid.

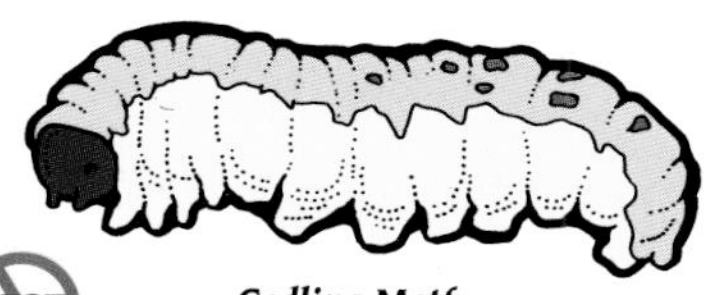

PEST *Codling Moth* (Carpocapsa pomonella)

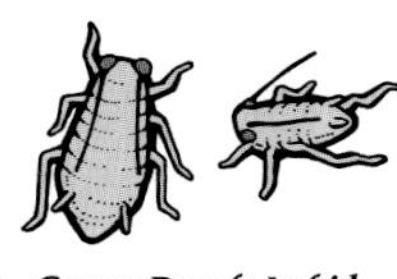

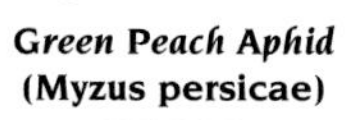

PEST *Green Peach Aphid* (Myzus persicae)

Other Environmentally Friendly Pest Controls

There are plant-derived, botanical controls, like rotenone and pyrethrum, available in dust and spray form. They degrade quickly, but take care of your pest problem effectively.

Bug-zapping light traps can capture flying plant predators, but they can be loud and annoying. You can easily spread sticky garden adhesive (available at most hardware or gardening stores) around tree trunks to discourage crawling pests.

PEST

Ant
(Family Formicidae)

Integrated Pest Management (I.P.M.)

Disney horticulturists believe in environmentally sound pest control practices and follow the philosophy of Integrated Pest Management (I.P.M.), where different methods of pest control are used for efficiency as well as economical results. The concept limits pesticide usage through alternative pest management practices. Each pest problem is analyzed independently and various cultural, biological, mechanical, and, if necessary, the least toxic chemical methods are used to eliminate the problem. If there are only a few insects on a plant, hand-picking is the answer. If the problem is more widespread, then a predatory pest or spraying with a horticultural soap or pesticide may be the solution.

Colorado Potato Beetle
(Leptinotarsa decemlineata)

Chemical Controls

If you must use chemical controls, take a sample of your sick plant(s) — or better yet, the actual pest — to the garden supply store and ask for their recommendations. Read the labels carefully and follow all directions. Certain chemicals can be very toxic, not only to the pests, but to people and pets, too. Be sure to store them safely as well.

Other Pests

Not all pests are insects. Caterpillars, slugs, and snails also enjoy dining on your tender plants, especially late at night when you're sleeping! If you awake one morning to see holes in your plant leaves, look under flower pots and other dark hiding places to catch the culprits. Set out slug bait to eliminate them quickly. If you don't have the heart to kill them, capture them when they're in their nightly feeding frenzy. Take a flashlight out after dark and collect all the snails, caterpillars, and slugs in a jar. Walk or drive somewhere and set them free in an open field where they can't do more damage.

Deer, rabbits, chipmunks, squirrels, gophers, mice, moles, and certain birds can also take their toll on your yard. They are a bit harder to control and a lot cuter than insects, too. Fences or netting helps in certain cases. A scarecrow can sometimes do the job. Anything that makes noise, like pie tins strung together and blowing in the breeze, scares many "big pests" away. There are also extremely effective scented repellent products on the market.

PEST

Snail
(Phylum: Mollusca)

Whatever methods you use to control pests in your landscape, think prevention and natural organic controls first.

Diseases

All living things, including plants, are susceptible to invasion by disease. Plants can be attacked by rust, scab, mildew, blight, anthracnose, and other equally awful sounding diseases. Remember, healthy plants are disease-resistant plants.

Most plant diseases, including bacterial, fungal, and viral, can be minimized by taking some preventive steps:

- ❑ Provide plants with proper growing conditions. Don't crowd mildew-prone plants together and don't locate sun-worshipping plants in the shade.
- ❑ Keep your garden weed-free and remove dead flowers and fallen fruit.
- ❑ Keep insects under control.
- ❑ Plant disease-resistant plant varieties.
- ❑ Remove diseased, old, or weak plants as soon as possible.
- ❑ Water and fertilize as necessary.
- ❑ Burn or discard diseased plants.

Garden Grooming

Weeding

Weeds compete with flowers and other plants for water, nutrients, and light. In flower beds, regular cultivation with a fork or three-pronged cultivator prevents weeds by exposing delicate weed seeds and seedlings to sun, drying them out before they can take root. Lightly scraping the top one inch of soil between the plants also helps deter soil compaction, introduces air back into the soil, and increases root development.

Applying a layer of mulch around the plants keeps weeds down, helps to retain moisture, and maintains soil and plant temperature. If you are changing a flower bed often, however, remember that mulches are sometimes difficult to remove and reuse. You should pull weeds around flowers by hand because herbicides shouldn't be used in flower beds. They will kill the flowers, too.

Pinching

Pinching, or "dead heading," is the removal of dead flower blossoms. This not only beautifies the plant, but encourages further blooming. Give your plants a good pinch once in a while and you'll soon see how much they like it! Flowers that respond well to pinching include petunia, marigold, pansy, and salvia. Certain flowers, like begonias and impatiens, are self-grooming and have so many blooms that removing dead blossoms is impractical.

Pruning

Trees and shrubs need pruning to stay healthy and in tip-top shape. Pruning is basically the removal of certain plant parts to create a specific shape, maintain a particular size, increase the production of flowers, fruit or branching, and maintain plant vitality. Pruning dead or dying limbs also decreases the chance of a branch falling on someone or something. Topiary and bonsai are dramatic examples of careful pruning.

You can prune for plant health and safety anytime of the year, but when pruning for shape and size, timing is important. Seasonally blooming plants like azalea and gardenia should be pruned after their peak bloom has finished. Deciduous trees, like maple and crape myrtle, should be pruned when dormant for maximum impact. Most evergreens can be pruned at anytime. Yellowing fronds, flower spikes, and "boots" can be groomed from palm trees throughout the year. Prune dead wood, suckers, and mature blooms from roses when they appear.

There are four basic pruning methods. **Heading back** is selectively removing the ends of twigs, shoots, or branches back to the axillary bud or node, creating a thick, formal-looking plant. **Thinning** is the removal of branches back to lateral branches, the

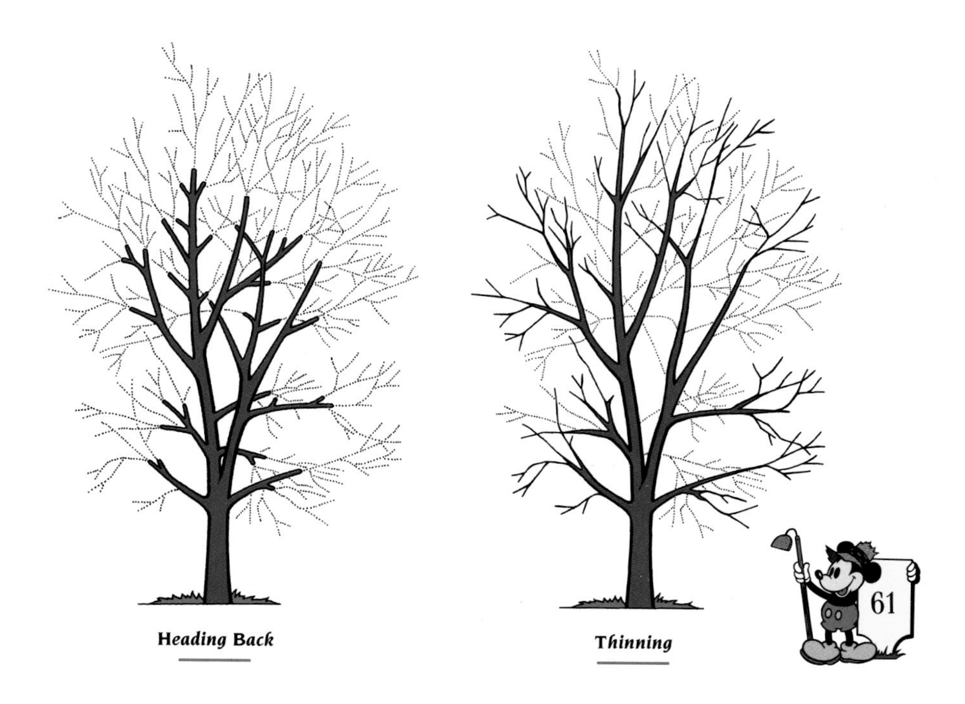

Heading Back *Thinning*

trunk, or the ground, and gives the tree a more open and natural appearance. **Shearing or shaping** is performed to encourage dense growth and to maintain formally shaped trees, shrubs, and topiary figures. **Skirting** a tree, the removal of lower branches, is usually executed to open up a view or keep dangerously low branches out of walkways.

Where you make the cuts is extremely important. You can't just randomly prune and expect the best results. It's important to cut just above a bud or a good branch, or make the cut against the trunk or base. If you leave even a small stub, nourishment will not pass through the tissue below the cut. The stub will wither and die, possibly creating a breeding ground for disease and killing the branch.

Learning to prune the plants in your landscape correctly can be one of your best investments in time and energy. The results are healthier and handsome plants and a yard that looks balanced and well manicured.

Shearing

Skirting

Gardening Environmentally

Living an environmentally friendly life is becoming a necessity for all of us. We're now quite accustomed to car pooling, safely disposing of our toxic chemicals, and recycling our newspapers, aluminum cans, plastics, and glass. Here are a few of the many environmentally safer gardening techniques you can practice:

Choose disease- and drought-resistant plants.

- ❑ Xeriscape with drought-tolerant plants or plants requiring minimal water to reduce water usage.
- ❑ Select disease- and pest-resistant varieties of plants to decrease the need for chemical controls.
- ❑ Use organic fertilizers rather than inorganic, manufactured chemical fertilizers.
- ❑ Use fiber pots that decompose instead of plastic pots.
- ❑ Recycle plastic pots.
- ❑ Use mulch.
- ❑ Recycle garden debris and certain organic kitchen waste products, such as vegetables, and coffee grounds, in a compost pile to use as a soil amendment.
- ❑ Practice Integrated Pest Management techniques.

Recycle vegetable waste in your compost pile.

Use fiber pots instead of plastic when possible.

TRIVIA

- Using waste wood, grass clippings, and sewage sludge, Walt Disney World Resort produces 40 to 50 cubic yards of compost (about five dump trucks worth) each day!

- Neem is a botanical pesticide that is extracted from seeds of a type of mahogany tree in India. The Disney Theme Parks and Resorts use neem in several ways: to repel some insects, sterilize others, and cause even others to loose their appetite!

- 1,000 tons of fertilizer are used each year at Walt Disney World Resort.

- 2,000 miles of irrigation pipe with 50,000 sprinkler heads and 292 automatic clocks controlled by a state-of-the-art centralized computer system keep everything watered at Walt Disney World Resort.

- Pesky flies from Australia, known as *psyllids*, were attacking the Austrialian bush cherry used at Disneyland Park for visual screening and topiary figures. A parasitic wasp, a natural predator of the psyllid, solved the problem in a bio-friendly fashion.

- At Disneyland Park, *pyrethrin* is a common botanical pesticide made from the petals of a species of chrysanthemum. This compound is used to reduce flying insects on Tom Sawyer Island.

Create
your landscap
with a
"painter's eye

To an artist, palette may refer to the range of colors used in a painting. To a gardener, palette refers to the many choices available to create a beautiful landscape. A gardener's palette consists of trees, flowers, shrubs, grass, ground covers, vines, and more. Each of these components also offers unique characteristics such as color, texture, shape, size, fragrance, and many other elements. When putting these pieces together, a gardener composes a "picture" and creates a landscape "painting."

A true landscape masterpiece is the result of careful planning, proper utilization of space, appropriate selection of plant materials, and conscientious maintenance.

Mounds of white flowers imitate snow at Canada in EPCOT.

Planning ahead is the key to success, whether you're starting from scratch at a brand-new house, revitalizing an overgrown jungle of weedy land, or simply adding a new tree to your front yard. You need to make your plant selections based on what you know about the total environment of your landscape, including the color and style of your home. Once you've done all your research, draw up your plans, make your lists, and get going!

Making Your Plan

Ask yourself what you want to achieve in your landscape. An area for private retreat? A colorful bed of flowers? An easy-care yard? A place for the kids to play? A personal sanctuary? An "instant" landscape? A disguise for an unsightly view? Maybe it's a combination of several ideas.

When designing your landscape, gather as much information as possible *before* making your plant selections. Study gardening books, collect magazine photos of gardening ideas you like, and take notes, make sketches or take photos of what looks nice in neighbors' yards. Many owners of beautifully landscaped yards are proud to share their green thumb secrets with fellow gardeners. Send for plant and seed catalogs and ask questions at local plant nurseries.

Then measure your yard or the area you want to landscape and make a "floor plan." Be sure to include walls patios, fences, swimming pools, woods, or any other boundaries. Try to add some curved lines to your plan, such as a circular planting of shrubs around a tree, a winding path of flowers along a fence, or a free-form herb garden.

Make a list of what existing plants will stay, determine which areas are shaded and which are in full sun. Take note of prevailing winds, what kind of soil you have, and any amendments you might need to make. Check the USDA Plant Hardiness Zone Map and choose plants appropriate to your zone.

Inspirational Sources

- Arboretums
- Botanical gardens
- Flower festivals
- Flower society shows
- Garden centers
- Garden clubs/classes
- Gardening books
- Gardening magazines
- Gardening sections of local newspapers/magazines
- Neighbors' yards
- Parks
- Seed catalogs
- TV gardening shows

Color Relationships

When deciding where to locate plants, don't forget about color relationships or the fact that you are composing a landscape "picture." Ask yourself what colors look good together, just as if you were selecting new furniture for the living room.

Tropical-looking plants add jungle ambiance at Mexico in EPCOT.

Don't just select those plants with the most vibrant colors, think in terms of complementary or contrasting colors that will harmonize with the environment you will be planting them in. Colors can create a focal point, drawing your eye toward a garden corner or diverting attention away from an eyesore if planted in another direction. They can enhance a theme or create a mood.

At Magic Kingdom Park, pink and white flowers accentuate the whimsical theme of Fantasyland. The wild west comes alive in Frontierland® with its meadow-like plantings of mixed annuals. Bright yellow and orange blossoms create a bold landscape in Future World. Adventureland®, Disney's Polynesian Resort, and Mexico in EPCOT are complemented by well-planned placement of luxuriant tropical foliage and exotic spots of color. The lavender, pink, and white color scheme of It's a Small World in Disneyland Park sets the stage for a mix of pink pastel pansies, primrose, and lavender stock in winter and spring.

Matching foliage and blossom color harmonize well.

The Color Wheel

A color wheel graphically demonstrates basic color interrelationships and is an easy way to help you select your garden colors and understand how these colors contrast and complement each other.

The color wheel also shows the distinction between "warm" and "cool" colors. The colors from yellow to red are considered warm colors. The colors from green to violet, the cool colors. The eyes see warm colors advance and cool colors recede. In other words, warm colors would appear to be closer to you than the cool colors if they were planted together. Mass plantings of cool colors can make a yard appear larger and, conversely, warm colors make the landscape seem more cozy. Cool colors are typically better for viewing up-close and warm colors for distant drama. Cool colors are more subtle in their impact than warm colors and can be easily overwhelmed by the dominating warm colors.

Red, yellow, and blue are considered "primary colors" because all the other colors can be produced by mixing them. The three midway points between the primary colors are green, orange, and violet. Colors on neighboring sides of each other, like red, red-violet, and violet, usually harmonize and those on the complete opposite side contrast.

For example, green and red, yellow and violet, orange and blue, are maximum contrasts and are considered "complementary" and really stand out when used together. Subordination, the method of selecting one color as the dominant color in a multicolored planting scheme, takes the fussiness out of bold contrasts and the tedium out of excessively harmonious color combinations.

Colorful chrysanthemums wind their way through Canada in EPCOT.

Polychromatic and Monochromatic Colors

A polychromatic color scheme, using any or all colors, can work beautifully in a garden. The result is a lively, happy, "riot" of color and activity. Although this seemingly haphazard selection of garden color is usually chalked up to inexperience, there are really no mistakes in nature. In fact, you may accidentally come up with a wonderful combination of color you like so much you repeat it for years to come.

The most dramatic and visually impressive landscape spectacles are often created with a monochromatic color scheme — the combination of various shades and tints of a single color. Of course, in reality, no floral display can be completely monochromatic because plant leaves and stems grow in various shades of green or brown. Fortunately, those shades become the perfect neutral backdrop for the monochromatic color scheme, not detracting from, but enhancing the whole dazzling effect.

Maximum color contrast increases visual excitement.

Delicate jacaranda blossoms form a radiant pastel canopy.

White is an elegant monochromatic color option and offers the most striking contrast against green foliage. Mounds of pure white-flowering plants on a hilly expanse can seem like billowing clouds reflecting the sunlight. White flowers, visible like softly glowing lamps in the moonlight, are very romantic, too. Imagine an evening stroll, arm-in-arm, through a path of heavenly fragrant white roses where fire flies glitter and delicate-winged moths flitter through the blossoms!

Remember, green is a color, too. You can compose a verdant monochromatic landscape using wonderfully textured foliage plants of varying heights and shades to create a "natural" garden or maybe even a mysterious, tropical jungle. Add visual interest by carrying the theme above ground level into lush hanging baskets, overflowing pots, and profusely planted window boxes.

For solid expanses of color, plant petunia, impatiens, chrysanthemum, alyssum, daisy, zinnia, tulip, daffodil, and Oriental poppy, depending upon what you can grow in your zone.

Red, white, and blue flowers add patriotic spirit at The American Adventure in EPCOT.

Flowers coordinate with architecture at United Kingdom in EPCOT.

Colors Create Emotions

Certain colors can elicit strong emotions. Soft blues, gentle mauves, and delicate violet shades are very soothing to the spirit and would be the appropriate choice for a tranquil backyard retreat. Pure white creates a sense of serenity, freshness, and formality like no other. Exuberant red and vibrant orange would set a pool party or backyard barbecue into high gear. Bright yellow cheers you up like the warm sunshine, just like seeing the first daffodil of spring!

A flowing, curving bed of blue, light blue, and violet-blue flowers can imitate a cool, bubbling stream where none exists. Scarlet petunias, snuggled closely together in a rectangular configuration,

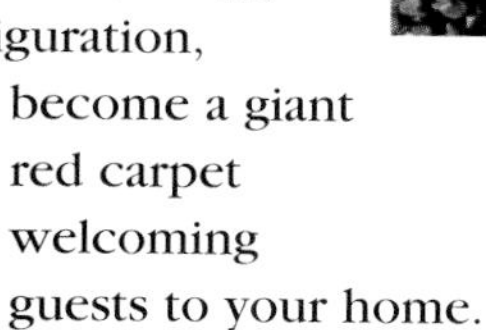

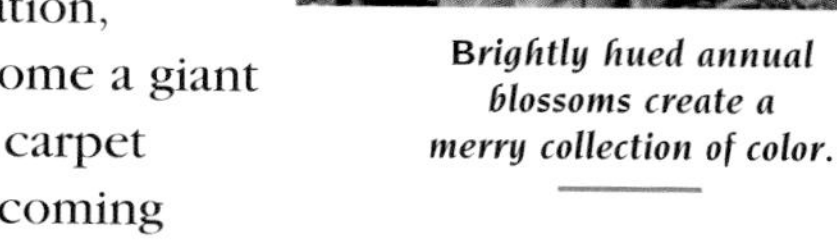

become a giant red carpet welcoming guests to your home.

Brightly hued annual blossoms create a merry collection of color.

Pink and red geraniums bloom at Disney Village Marketplace.

Berries and foliage provide additional color accents in the landscape.

Landscape Color Options

Don't overlook the exciting color that can also come from the foliage, blossoms, fruits, and berries of trees, vines, and shrubs. Many varieties have variegated leaves with stripes and dots of pleasant color. On some plants, new growth starts out red or light green, and changes as it matures. Many trees and shrubs also change their color and appearance with the seasons.

There is an almost infinite variety of floral, foliage, bark, and fruit color in nature. Take advantage of this seemingly endless spectrum by experimenting in your own landscape to create an unforgettable display. To complete the setting, incorporate coordinating lawn furniture, awnings, planters, and umbrellas into your setting. Now you get the idea!

Bold, variegated color dapples the leaves of this croton.

Gardener's Palette

Things to Consider Before Planting

- ❑ Plants grow, changing in height and width. Will a mature version of a plant always fit into your landscape?
- ❑ Some plants change their appearance with the seasons. Do you mind bare limbs or raking?
- ❑ Certain plants require special or excessive maintenance. Do you have time to provide constant care?
- ❑ Some plants are more prone to pests and disease. Are you ready to do battle?

A curving bed of bright annuals highlights the Hub in Magic Kingdom Park.

Instant Landscaping

Have you ever noticed that everything is in full bloom when you're at any of the Walt Disney Theme Parks and Resorts? You probably thought, "What a stroke of luck to be here when the flowers look so beautiful." Actually, careful planning, computers, a massive amount of manual labor, and over two million bedding plants a year at Walt Disney World Resort alone, go into maintaining this year-round impression.

"Instant landscaping," in Disney terms, is the selection and planting of mature plants, flowers, shrubs, sod, and trees to create the immediate appearance of a lushly growing landscape, to provide scale to the surroundings, and to establish a certain ambiance and unique character to the landscape.

Salvia, lantana, and marigold are sun-loving favorites.

The instant landscaping philosophy began in 1954 when Walt Disney told landscape architect Bill Evans to prepare the planting plans. Walt told Bill, "Disneyland must be a show from the opening day." This philosophy has been observed in all the Walt Disney Theme Parks and Resorts since that day, much to the delight of guests.

Poinsettias enliven the holiday cheer in Disney's Grand Floridian Beach Resort.

For example, when EPCOT opened in 1982, 72 Disney gardeners transformed approximately 600 acres from sand brown to lush green. On the west bank of CommuniCore (now the location of Innoventions) they planted 100 full-sized trees and five acres of grassy turf in only 10 hours!

In our everyday lives, we see evidence of instant landscaping all around us. When new homes are built, large trees, shrubs, sod, and blooming flowers are added, not only to replenish the plant materials torn from the ground during construction, but also to provide that "welcome home" feeling. Instant landscaping is often used when someone is trying to sell a home to give it "curb appeal." Even a ho-hum yard can become a blooming showplace in just a few hours.

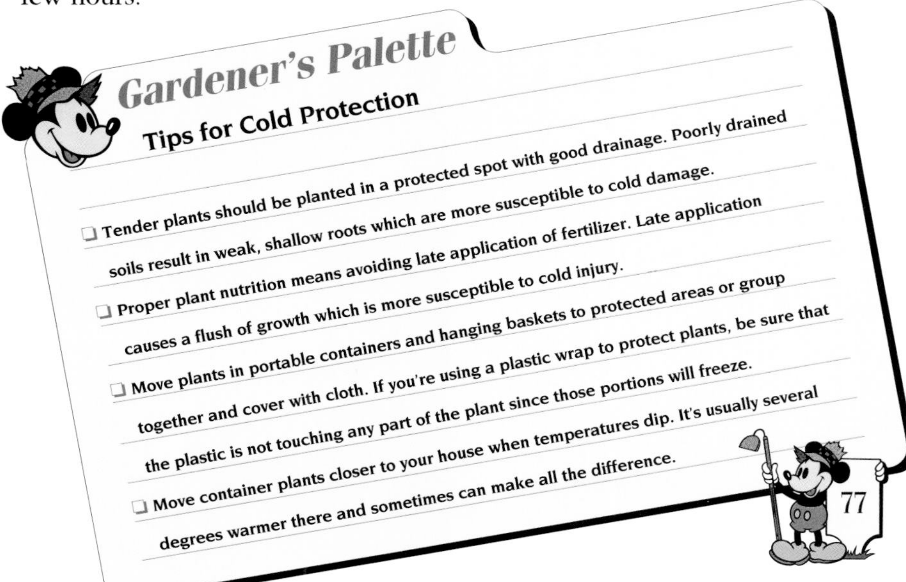

Spaceship **Earth** *in* **EPCOT** *towers behind a fully blooming crape myrtle.*

Trees

Trees are the backbone of your garden. They are one of the most important elements in landscaping, and certainly the most prominent, permanent, and three-dimensional plants in a landscape.

Trees are used for protection from sun, wind, and rain, and at other times to create a beautiful backdrop, to soften architectural lines, to screen out an unappealing view, or to provide privacy. Some trees are planted for their vivid colors, unusual shapes, showy flowers, exotic fragrances, or interesting textures, berries, or bark. In fact, some bark is so peculiar many gardeners think they have a pest problem! For example, the twigs of the sweet gum tree are often covered with unusual cork-like ridges that some people mistake for scale insects. Other trees have bark which is chunky, smooth, cracked, peeled, blotchy, or furrowed in appearance.

Trees can enhance and create a mood — tropical, formal, whimsical, romantic, inviting, cosmopolitan, peaceful, old-fashioned, and beyond. With a little imagination you can create an exciting, new "environment" in your landscape.

A single large tree, like an oak, can make an impressive visual statement, but remember it takes years to attain its massive size. Certain trees can become a dramatic design feature when planted in groupings of three or four. Trees planted in groupings can also become a fence, a windbreak, a shady tunnel, a place to hang a hammock or build a cozy picnic area, or even a living sculpture. Trees planted in a symmetrical layout give the landscape a balanced and planned look and asymmetrical plantings provide a natural, enchanting, or casual appearance.

Evergreen Italian cypress soar at Italy in **EPCOT.**

Evergreen Trees

Evergreen, as the name implies, refers to the group of trees with foliage that remains green throughout the year. Broad-leaved evergreen trees, like holly, southern magnolia, and live oak trees, have thick masses of foliage and create outstanding vistas when planted together as specimen groups, or grown as borders or screens. Coniferous evergreens (trees which produce cones), such as cedar, fir, cypress, pine, and spruce trees, are often planted as backdrops for small flowering trees, shrubs, and flower beds, and used for screens or windbreaks. Coniferous evergreens are also excellent stand-alone trees and many birds seek shelter and make their homes in the dense greenery.

Deciduous Trees

Deciduous trees (those that lose their foliage after the growing season) come in a wide and interesting variety of shapes and sizes. Popular deciduous trees include ash, beech, birch, maple, and willow. Some grow in spreading or vase shapes and provide a large canopy of shade, decreasing the need for air conditioning throughout the summer. Some develop into a weeping configuration, spreading their roots as wide as their height. Others grow in tall columns and make imposing hedges that can effectively block the wind, screen out a view, line a long driveway, or define a property line. Several mature into pyramid form, taking on a rather stately and formal appearance that lend themselves nicely to lawn plantings.

In autumn, many deciduous trees come alive in a vivid burst of color, and in the winter, leafless deciduous trees add interesting silhouettes to the twilight skyline with their stark branches. In the winter, a bare tree allows early morning sunlight to reach the roof, warming the house and decreasing the amount of time the furnace needs to run.

Certain flowering deciduous trees gaily welcome spring with their bouquets of colorful blossoms. These flowering deciduous trees, like the dogwood, flowering cherry, and crab apple, are nearly everyone's favorites with their breathtaking beauty, and in some cases, captivating fragrance. Birds and other wildlife are also attracted to the many flowering trees which produce fruit. Songbirds especially like the Japanese or Kousa dogwood. Although most flowering deciduous trees bloom in spring, the Japanese pagoda tree, sorrel tree, and the yellowwood bloom in mid- to late summer.

Date Palms Get a Second Chance in Disney-MGM Studios Theme Park

A date production farm in Indio, California was about to remove date palms *(Phoenix dactylifera)* out of production because of changes in market demand for the particular variety they had been growing. Also, these 30-foot giants had grown too tall for farm workers to easily maintain and harvest. In date production, a grove of 500 female palms is hand-pollinated from a single male tree. A considerable amount of time was being expended just scaling these "towers." Being resourceful and appreciative of the grandeur of such specimen trees, a deal was struck to transport 16 hand–selected behemoths to Florida. Twelve of them now grace the Animation Courtyard and four are expertly replanted in front of the Academy of Television Arts and Sciences at Disney-MGM Studios Theme Park.

Mickey's Favorite Flowering Trees

Acacia *(Acacia baileyana)*
African Tulip Tree
(Spathodea campanulata)

Bottle Brush *(Callistemon)*
Brisbane Box *(Tristania conferta)*
Caribbean Copper Plant
(Euphorbia cotinifolia)

Chinese Flame Tree
(Koelrueteria bipinatus)

Coral Tree *(Erythrina)*
Crape Myrtle
(Lagerstroemia indica)
Evergreen Pear *(Pyrus kawakamii)*
Firewheel Tree
(Stenocarpus sinautus)

Floss Silk Tree *(Chorisia speciosa)*
Frangipani *(Plumeria)*
Fringe Tree *(Chionanthus retusa)*
Giant Thevetia
(Thevetia thevetiodes)

Gold Medallion Tree
(Cassia leptophylla)

Golden Fragrance
(Pittosporum napaulense)

Golden Trumpet Tree
(Tabebuia chrysotricha)

Golden Wonder Senna
(Cassia splendida)

Hong Kong Orchid Tree
(Bauhinia blakeana)

Horse Chestnut
(Calodendron capense)

Jacaranda *(Jacaranda acutifolia)*
Magnolia *(Magnolia grandiflora)*
Mexican Palo Verde
(Parkinsonia aculeata)

Moreton Bay Chestnut
(Castanospermum australe)

Pink Ball Dombeya
(Dombeya cacuminum)

Pink Iron Bark
(Eucalyptus sideroxylon)

Poinciana *(Caesalpinia spinosa)*
Purple Orchid Tree
(Bauhinia variegata)

Red Flowering Gum
(Eucalyptus ficifolia)

Silk Oak Tree
(Grevillea robusta)

Silk Tree or Mimosa
(Albizia julibrissin)

Sweetshade
(Hymenosporum flavum)

Tipu Tree *(Tipuana tipu)*
Trumpet Tree *(Tabebuia)*

Selecting Your Trees

Drive through your area and observe what other people have planted or visit an arboretum, if there is one near you. Take a camera with you so you can identify the tree types later. Take note of where and how the trees are situated in the landscape and what other plantings accentuate the total picture. Think about your own yard and what types and shapes of trees would best fit into the landscape.

Consider planting a flowering tree outside a living room, dining room or family room window you look out often. By doing so, you'll reap year 'round benefits, including colorful blooms, interesting foliage and bark, delicate fragrance, and a spectacular wildlife show.

You can cut your heating and cooling costs by planting trees in certain locations, too. Evergreens planted on the north and west side of your house will help shield you from bitter winter winds. Deciduous trees situated on the south, east, or west sides of your home will shade you from the heat of summer and in winter, when their branches are bare, will allow the warm sunshine to flood into your windows.

Certain trees, like weeping willows and poplars, can interfere with underground utilities and pipes, foundations, and swimming pools, and need to be planted at a proper distance. Other trees eventually grow to mammoth size and prevent light from reaching your home and lawn. Whatever trees you plant, choose carefully.

Ask yourself the following questions when selecting a tree:

- ❑ Where will the tree fit in my landscape?
- ❑ What is the tree's growth rate?
- ❑ What is the tree's eventual size?
- ❑ Will the tree block any views when it reaches maturity?
- ❑ What shape will the tree grow into?
- ❑ What color leaves and bark does the tree have?
- ❑ What will the tree's proximity be to other trees, plants, or buildings?
- ❑ Will the tree drop its leaves?
- ❑ How much time do I have to spend on maintenance (like raking, pruning, fertilizing, etc.)?

Planting Trees

You should always plant the best-quality nursery stock available because spending a few extra dollars at planting time will produce much sturdier and healthier trees in the years to come. Look for trees with straight trunks, strong, well-spaced branches, and lush, nicely shaped foliage. Avoid trees with signs of disease, bruised or damaged bark, wilting, insect activity, or a tangle of roots coming out the top of the container. Your local plant nursery or county agricultural extension agent can suggest which trees are appropriate for your climate and answer your questions.

A large, spreading tree can become a welcome umbrella of shade.

Most often, trees come "balled-and-burlapped," or "B & B." The tree is dug up while dormant and the root ball is wrapped in jute or burlap. Although this is a popular method of providing trees for transplant, new research indicates this is very stressful to the tree because much of the root area can be lost during the "B & B" process. Sometimes trees are sold bare root, but more often you now find trees grown in 3- to 7-gallon (or larger) containers.

Balled-and-burlapped trees get acclimated more quickly if planted in early spring or early fall, but can be planted at any time during the growing season. Plant a bare-root tree in early spring as soon as you can work the soil and while the plant is still dormant. You can plant a container-grown tree anytime during the growing season, but certain experts agree that you can give your tree a head start in spring and beat the summer heat and cold winter air by planting in early fall.

Planting Distances

Some trees, like palm and birch, are suitable for grouping, but others need more space. Small flowering trees and dwarf fruit trees should be planted at least 8' from buildings and approximately 10' from other plants. Large trees with wide, spreading branches often grow roots and branches as wide as their heights and need 65' between trunks to develop properly. Space nonspreading trees 35' apart so their naturally growing forms are undisturbed. Spreading trees planted with nonspreading trees compete for nutrients, moisture, and light and need to be planted 45' apart.

How to Plant a Tree

What You'll Need

- ❑ A container-grown or balled-and-burlapped tree
- ❑ Shovel
- ❑ Top soil or fertile loam (optional)
- ❑ Knife

1. Dig a hole at least 2' wider than the root ball. If you have compacted or other poor soil conditions, dig the hole even wider, b not deeper.

2. Check your drainage by filling the hole wi water and letting it stand over night. If all the water hasn't drained by the next day, you'll have to elevate the grade of the planting site, plant the tree in a higher location, or provide better drainage with a perforated pipe. (Perforated pipe method: Dig a trench that aims down and away fro the hole and lay a length of perforated pip that drains into a dry well or a similar-type opening. Replace soil.)

3. If the soil from the hole is mostly clay, replace it with high quality topsoil. If the soil is very sandy or full of gravel, mix in about one-third fertile loam with the backfill soil. Remove any rocks and break up any chunks of soil. Current research indicates adding amendments, like manur or fertilizer, during planting time are not necessary.

4

Just before planting, remove containers from container-grown plants and any plastic or cords from B & B trees. If your tree roots are wrapped in burlap you can leave it in place because it will rot away. If your container-grown plant appears pot-bound, score the root ball vertically with a sharp knife to a depth of about $\frac{1}{8}$" every 2" to 3". This step stimulates outward root growth.

5

Place the root ball in the hole. Backfill the hole about half way with soil and gently, yet firmly, press the soil to eliminate any air pockets. Water thoroughly and let the water soak in. Backfill the hole completely and build a rim around the top edge to make a saucer-shaped indention. Fill the saucer with water and allow it to soak in overnight. Refill the saucer the next day.

Tree Care After Planting

During the tree's first year, watch the water supply very carefully. In dry times or in areas with high temperatures, water thoroughly every five to seven days, or as necessary. Newly planted trees often need staking to hold them upright and to prevent wind damage. The staking method must allow for some motion to assure that the trunk and roots will become strong and sturdy.

Mulch all trees with pine needles, bark chips, gravel, or leaves to prevent excessive moisture loss, and reduce competition from grass and weeds for nutrients. Spread the mulch evenly around the tree at a point starting from about 6" from the trunk in a circular area of 2' to 3'. The mulch should be 3" to 4" deep.

Fertilize the mulched area two or three times during the first and second growing seasons with a commercial fertilizer, manure, or another high-nitrogen organic fertilizer.

Trees line Rivers of America in Disneyland Park.

How to Stake a Tree

What You'll Need

- ❑ 1 pressure-treated 2" x 2" stake, 6' to 8' tall depending on tree height
- ❑ Sledge hammer
- ❑ #12-gauge galvanized steel wire
- ❑ 2 to 3 turnbuckles
- ❑ 2 to 3 plastic tie friction guards

1 Use the sledge hammer to drive the stake down alongside the root ball, into the ground to at least one-third its total length.

2 Use enough wire to wrap once around the stake and tree. Be sure to slip on the friction guards. Wrap loosely around the tree to prevent girdling.

3 Fasten wires together with turnbuckles. Leave the stake in place for six months to one year.

Tree Pests and Diseases

Prevention is the best medicine for trees, too. If you give a tree proper growing conditions, including the right light, water, soil, and exposure, your problems should be minimal. But if you discover some pesky rascal devouring your tree or hideous black mold covering the foliage, you may have to get tough!

Certain insects can defoliate trees, suck tree sap, wither foliage, stunt growth, and even kill whole trees if not stopped in their tracks. If you can, trap one of the predators in a plastic bag (leaf or branch and all) and take it to your local garden store or agricultural extension agency. They will be able to determine which pest it is and advise you on the best methods for control.

Many tree diseases mimic insect infestation with wilted, distorted, or discolored foliage. Some diseases cause blotches on the leaves, falling twigs, bark lesions, and even branch death. Sometimes fungicides are effective, occasionally pruning out the infected branches works, and other times, complete removal of the tree is necessary. Again, as with insect problems, bring a sample of the damage and a good description of the problem to a professional and ask for advice.

Gardener's Palette

Common Tree Pests & Diseases

PESTS	DISEASES
Aphids	Anthracnose
Borers	Cytospora Canker
Caterpillars	Fire Blight
Lace Bugs	Juniper Blight
Leaf Miners	Rust
Leaf-skeletonizing Beetles	Sphaeropsis Tip Blight
Pine Bark Beetles	Verticullium Wilt
Scales	
Spider Mites	

Redwoods in Florida?! True Wonders of Nature Grow in Disney-MGM Studios Theme Park

Redwoods, typically associated with northern California, were chosen by Disney Imagineers and gardeners to represent the giant trees of the fictional Star Tours planet of Endor.

Disney horticulturists were skeptical about growing real redwoods in a warm, humid climate, due to a previous unsuccessful experience trying to grow redwoods in 1969 in Magic Kingdom Park. The native Florida bald cypress *(Taxodium distichum)* was proposed as a look-alike, but, unfortunately they are not as evergreen as redwoods. Fortunately, a special last-minute discovery offered an exciting and challenging alternative.

There were a number of unique container-grown redwoods at a nursery near Gilroy, California that specializes in unusual trees. A special cultivar, *Sequoiadendron sempervirens* 'Aptos Blue,' was suggested and selected for its ability to tolerate warm weather like that in Florida. These container-grown plants were used to a particular regimen of watering and fertilization, so specific cultural requirements were necessary for successful growth in Florida.

Disney gardeners quickly accepted the challenge and went to work to provide special irrigation, drainage, and soil to duplicate the conditions the trees had become accustomed to.

The trees now grow at the entrance of the Star Tours attraction. The final touch was a fog system simulating the native environment of redwoods in northern California and the other-worldly look of another planet.

Big Tree Moving Success Stories

Years ago, a 130-year-old live oak tree was discovered growing on the south end of the Walt Disney World Resort property. It weighed 38 tons and had a root ball measuring 18' by 16' by 14' deep. This massive tree now grows year by year in the heart of Liberty Square in Magic Kingdom Park. But how did it get there?

Well, months of tender loving care, a 100-ton crane (that nearly tipped during transplanting), one extensively damaged (then repaired) bridge, meticulous pruning, and two 2" holes drilled through the tree trunk and fitted with case-hardened steel dowel pins are only part of the story.

The rest of the plot includes special road clearances, the temporary removal of power lines, a gigantic hole to accommodate the huge tree, and a half dozen arrestors that protect the massive oak from lightning strikes.

The tree was fittingly named the Disney "Liberty Tree." The oak, as history tells us, was a symbol of challenge to the "tyrannie of King George III." After the Boston Tea Party of 1773, the Sons of Liberty hung lanterns of freedom from the "Liberty Tree," representing the 13 colonies forming the United States after the American Revolution. Disney horticulturists were so proud of their transplanting success story, they adopted the Liberty Tree as their official logo. But that's not the end of the story....

In recent years, an even bigger tree was successfully transplanted at the Ol' Man Island recreation area at Disney's Dixie Landings Resort. This oak tree weighs 85 tons, is estimated to be 100 to 200 years old, soars 55' into the air, and spreads 78' wide. This was no small feat. The transplanting endeavor required hundreds of workers, a 10-axle trailer, the moving of 108 power poles and six traffic signals, the crossing of five bridges, and a journey of 12 miles at four miles an hour. The estimated cost: somewhere near $1 million.

Shrubs

Shrubs are the garden workhorse of the plant palette. They are generally dependable growers, require minimal care, harmonize with the entire landscape, can add both color and fragrance, disguise an unwanted view, and maximize privacy. They can quickly soften the look of a barren yard and make it a lot more inviting.

Shrubs provide visual appeal all year, whether they're green and leafy, fully blooming, in an autumn show of color, fruit-covered, or leafless and angular in a wintry setting. A living wall of shrubs can quiet the sounds from a busy street and, when planted on a northern-facing wall, help deflect frigid winter wind. They can also accent an architectural aspect of your home. Some shrubs, particularly thorny varieties, can offer some security if planted under windows.

Types of Shrubs

There are three basic kinds of shrubs — deciduous, broad-leaved evergreens, and conifers (or narrow-leaved evergreens). Each type offers a variety of shapes, textures, and sizes. Some grow low. Others take on a rounded, compact shape. Certain shrubs grow tall and erect, many spread, and a few have elegant arching branches. Many types show-off with an abundance of spectacular flowers or a bounty of colorful berries. Some grow quickly and need regular pruning and others grow more slowly and need little maintenance.

Shrubs furnish woodsy atmosphere at Tom Sawyer Island in Magic Kingdom Park.

Selecting Shrubs

A practical approach to choosing shrubs is to decide what purpose they will serve. If you want to create a privacy screen, it's most logical to purchase some sort of evergreen shrubs that retain their foliage all year. If you have a small front yard and a tiny house and plant tall-growing evergreens as a barrier to the sidewalk or road, the house may end up looking like a fortress. You may also feel a bit claustrophobic each time you open the front door. Select shrubs you can easily prune to a more attractive height or those that only grow to a manageable size and in scale to your home if planting close to the house. Tall, dense evergreen shrubs are best suited for the outer boundaries of your property lines or where you need an effective wind barrier.

Shrubs can make a wonderful backdrop for a flower bed, particularly when the shrubs also blossom. You can plant a row of shrubs along a windowless expanse of wall or a foundation to soften a stark appearance. Shrubs with arching, fountain-like branches, like forsythia, make perfect specimen plantings all by themselves.

Accent a doorway with tall, upright shrubs and plant low- or medium-height shrubs under windows. Low-growing or spreading shrubs take centerstage in a front border. Spreading shrubs growing along a steep slope not only look good, they help prevent soil erosion, too. Ask your county agricultural extension agent or garden center staff what shrubs are available for your area and what cultural requirements they need for best growth.

An interesting mix of shrub type, texture, and height borders the **Disneyland Hotel.**

Common Broad-leaved Evergreen Shrubs

Abelia
Andromeda
Azalea *(not deciduous in mild areas like southern California and Florida)*
Black Barberry
Boxwood
Camellia
Carolina Rhododendron
Chinese Privet
Crimson Bottlebrush
Daphne
David Viburnum
Escallonia
Eugenia
Firethorn

Gardenia
Glossy Privet
Heather
Hibiscus *(not deciduous in mild areas like southern California and Florida)*
Holly
Indian Hawthorn
Japanese Laurel
Myrtle
Oleander
Photina
Pittosporum
Sacred Bamboo
Xylosma

Common Deciduous Shrubs

Beautybush
Crape Myrtle
Dwarf Horse Chestnut
Elderberry
Euonymus
Forsythia
Hydrangea
Japanese Barberry
Lilac
Mock Orange
Quince
Pussywillow
Rose-of-Sharon
Spirea

Shrub Planting and Maintenance

Like many plants, shrubs may be purchased in bare-root, balled-and-burlapped, or container-grown form. Follow the recommended planting, pruning, and fertilizing recommendations from nursery personnel or the directions on the plant tag for the best results.

Shrubs, with the exception of most deciduous types, need some pruning to look their best. Proper pruning can discourage disease and insect infestations by promoting better air circulation and increased access to sunlight. It can also encourage new growth and flowering. You should also prune shrubs to remove dead branches, give them a more appealing shape, or keep them from growing too large for the surroundings. Shrubs sheared into formally shaped hedges will obviously require more frequent care to keep them from looking ragged.

Ochna Serrulata: The Mickey Mouse Plant

Mickey Mouse has a namesake! This unusual evergreen shrub produces beautiful yellow flowers in early summer and eventually, the sunny-colored petals fall to the ground. Then the sepals (the green outer ring of floral parts) turn bright red and five or more green seed-like fruits project from the center. When these fruits later turn shiny black against the contrasting red of the sepals, many people swear they see the bright eyes and big ears of Mickey Mouse.

The shrub grows slowly, spreading out and reaching heights and widths of 4' to 8'. The leathery, oblong leaves grow from 2" to 5" long and are bronze-colored in the spring, turning deep green later in the season.

The Mickey Mouse plant is originally from exotic Natal (the tiniest province in South Africa) and is sometimes referred to as the Bird's-eye Bush. The shrub prefers partial shade, slightly acidic soil, and is fairly drought tolerant once it has been growing awhile. Sometimes people are able to grow them as indoor plants, but most often you find them growing in tubs or trained as small ornamental espaliers in temperate and subtropical zones 9 and 10.

Lawns

A lawn is an often over-looked gardening element because it's "just there." In reality, the green carpet of turf acts as a unifying ingredient, providing a neutral backdrop for the flowers, trees, paths, and the multitude of textures, shapes, colors, and other components comprising the entire landscape.

Grass is a soft and resilient outdoor floor, drawing our eyes as well as our feet in every direction it goes. It can be an inviting place to have a picnic, take a nap, or play volleyball. Freshly mown grass has a pleasantly unmistakable fragrance that seems to hang in the air. A lawn also acts as a natural air conditioner and a cool haven for bare feet running from hot cement.

Turf and Ornamental Grasses

Throughout Walt Disney Theme Parks and Resorts, specific types of turf grasses are selected for a variety of ornamental, recreational, and functional purposes. Zoysia grass carpets the pavilion areas of Future World and World Showcase in EPCOT, creating a lush green background, preventing soil erosion, and reducing glare from walkways and buildings. Sturdy hybrid Bermuda grasses are planted on the Walt Disney World Resort golf courses to withstand the heavy recreational usage and precise and frequent maintenance requirements. In Disneyland Park, the predominant grass used in turf areas is tall fescue. It's green all year, can withstand a certain amount of shade and foot traffic, and is tolerant of turf diseases.

Ornamental grass enhances landscape realism at China in EPCOT.

Along the unirrigated areas of roadways, canals, and lakes at Walt Disney World Resort, bahia grass aids in preventing erosion, dust, and mud problems. At the Resorts, reliable St. Augustine is the grass of choice for its all-around good looks and durability.

Disney horticulturists also select certain grasses to coordinate with a particular theme of an area. The Frontierland Train Station in the Magic Kingdom Park is surrounded by coarse-textured St. Augustine grass to emphasize a more rugged era in history. In the Hub area, delicate-textured hybrid Bermuda grass complements ornate Victorian parterre gardens. In Disneyland Park, the miniature lawns in Storybook Land are planted with zoysia, Bermuda, mondo grass, blue sedge, tufted hair grass, dwarf reed, and Little Bunny Fountain grass.

Some grasses take on multipurpose duties with a bit of alternative maintenance. For example, zoysia grass is allowed to grow long in the Wonders of Life pavilion in EPCOT, taking on a natural, wind-blown, meadow-like appearance.

Jungle Cruise creatures pose amidst ornamental grasses in Disneyland Park.

Many different types of grasses are planted around Splash Mountain in Disneyland Park for "special effects." Voluminous clumps of dechampsia grass are allowed to grow rampant and produce seed heads, giving the area a rocky meadow-like appearance. *Milla biflora,* a shorter, finer-textured grass is used for mounding. Large seed heads of "Fairy's Joke" hang above the winding water route like grassy waterfalls as guest float by underneath in log boats.

When selecting your grass, consider soil type, how much traffic or recreational usage the lawn will have to endure, what zone you are in, disease resistance, how much maintenance is required, and what "look" you're aiming for. Take into account any environmental stresses, too. If you live in an area plagued by drought or in a particularly soggy or exceptionally steep location, you'll have to select your grasses accordingly.

Seeding, Sodding, Plugging, and Sprigging

Bermuda grass carpets Eagle Pines Golf Course at Walt Disney World Resort.

If you're starting from scratch on bare soil, you need to grade the area as level as possible and make sure there is adequate drainage. Slope the soil gently away from your home to ensure no flooding. Remove any rocks, weeds, roots, or other debris. Most grasses prefer a neutral or slightly acidic pH level of 6 or 7. Test your soil and add lime (if necessary) to improve the soil environment and provide a better chemical balance. Then add peat, compost, and extra topsoil, if needed, for good growth.

Next, spread a complete fertilizer, such as 10-10-10 across the entire area at a rate of 10 to 20 pounds per 1,000 square feet. Till the soil to a depth of 6" to 8" and then rake smooth. Now you're ready to seed, sod, plug, or sprig.

Seeding grass seed can be tricky. When you're at the garden supply store, ask questions and be sure to read the package label. Check the germination rate, what grass varieties are included, and what percent inert matter is contained in the bag. The germination rate refers to what percentage of the seed will sprout successfully. Inert matter is the filler material used to ensure more effective broadcast coverage. Higher priced seed is often worth the price because you don't have to reseed later.

In many areas, early September or early spring is the best time to sow grass seed because cool season grasses tend to germinate best in temperatures of 60° to 70°. In southern climates, bahia and centipede warm season grasses are often used for seeding.

"Desert" grass adds **Old West** *authenticity to* **Frontierland** *in* **Magic Kingdom Park.**

A hand-operated, spinner-type spreader is the simplest method for sowing the seeds. Simply add the seeds to the spreader per package directions and spread half the seeds over the area going in one direction, then the other half in perpendicular fashion over the same area. Then gently rake to cover the seeds about 1/8". Roll the area with a drum roller (inexpensive to rent) and mulch very lightly with straw or peat moss to conserve moisture. The number one killer of newly planted lawns is dryness, so water very gently several times a day for the first week being careful not to disrupt the seeds. Water at least once a day for the following week and then less often as the grass becomes established.

Sodding is the preferred method for starting lawns in Walt Disney Theme Parks and Resorts because it offers that "instantly landscaped" appearance. Bermuda, centipede, St. Augustine, and zoysia are favorite grasses in Walt Disney World Resort. Sod is typically purchased in rectangular rolled or flat sections of already established grass and needs to be planted soon after purchase to avoid excessive drying. To sod your yard, prepare the soil using the same techniques as for seeding. Lay the sod, in staggered fashion rather than in perfectly straight lines, for a more natural appearance. Then roll and water the sod using the same techniques as for sowing with seed. At Walt Disney World Resort, a top dressing of sand is applied and then watered in to prevent the seams of the sod from drying out.

Plugging a lawn is essentially planting small pieces of sod in polka dot intervals across the soil. Runners form and spread out, rapidly filling in the bare soil. Bermuda, St. Augustine, and zoysia grass are often used as plugs. **Sprigging** involves taking rooted stem sections of grass and planting them 6" to 12" apart. They eventually spread and fill in to create a luxurious lawn. Rapidly establishing newly planted grass is important to prevent soil loss from wind and water erosion and to prevent weeds from taking over. It's also best to avoid walking on the grass until it's well established. Allow the grass to grow to a height of about 2", then mow to a height of 1½" and apply a light application of fertilizer. Fertilize lightly each month for the next three or four months.

Revitalizing Your Lawn

Grass is wonderfully resilient. Before you tear out your old lawn in frustration, try a few renovative tricks. Fall is the best time for these tasks in the North and in early spring for Southern lawns.

Start by raking up any leaves or other debris to give your grass some fresh air and sunshine. Then assess the weed situation. Control them first by removing as many as you can by hand. If necessary, apply an herbicide according to package directions.

If your grass has bare spots, it's time to reseed. Turn the soil over to a depth of 4" to 6" and add in some balanced fertilizer. Level the area with a rake and sow the seed across the surface. Gently press the seed into the soil about ⅛" and lightly mulch and water. Follow the same watering schedule as for seeding.

Sometimes an excessive amount of thatch can be a problem. Thatch is all the accumulated grass clippings, leaves, and other debris that forms a mat in the grass. A thick carpet of thatch (¾"+) can be an insect breeding ground, prevent new grass from sprouting, and prohibit fertilizer and water from getting where it's needed. A thinner mat of thatch can be beneficial because it stops some weeds from growing, decomposes to provide organic fertilizer, and recycles plant tissues. You can remove thatch (called verticutting) from a lawn with a power rake (these can be rented), raking energetically and deeply with a garden rake, or by applying a thatch-removing fertilizer or spray.

A good time to overseed and rejuvenate a lawn is right after dethatching. Overseed your lawn by spreading grass seed at half the rate recommended for seeding a new lawn. Usually this rate is one or two pounds per 1,000 square feet. In no time you'll see new grass.

Maybe your lawn looks a bit yellow or doesn't seem to be growing and needs a shot of fertilizer. Try to maintain a timely feeding schedule for a nice, healthy lawn that stays green. Refer to your grass seed package directions for recommended feedings.

Maintenance

A good, consistent maintenance routine will be rewarded with a healthy lawn that is resistant to diseases, pests, weeds, and environmental stresses. Disney gardeners owe their flourishing grasses to proper mowing, watering, fertilizing, aerating, and verticutting practices.

There are 1,500 acres of turf area in Walt Disney World Resort, including finely manicured lawns, miles of roadside turf, and golf courses. At three mowings each week, that adds up to 350,000 mowing miles per year — equivalent to 14 trips around the earth at the Equator!

Before the invention of the mechanical lawnmower in 1820, our gardening ancestors relied on scythes, sickles, and hungry sheep to keep their grass in check. Today you can choose from a wide selection of push mowers, self-propelled mowers, riding mowers, and even tractor mowers to easily take care of unruly turf.

In most areas, mowing once a week during the active growth season should be enough. In some places more frequent mowing is required. One rule of thumb is to not cut the grass more than one-third of its height. Keep your mower blades sharp so they cut — not tear — the grass. Cut the grass less frequently and about ½" higher in shady areas. During times of extreme heat or drought, cut the whole lawn higher to help conserve moisture. If you cut the grass regularly, the short clippings will decompose quickly. If you wait until the grass is long, you should bag or rake up the clippings and add them to your compost pile.

Gardener's Palette

Suggested Mowing Heights for Grasses

❑ Bahia Grass	2" to 3"
❑ Bent Grass	3/4" to 2"
❑ Common Bermuda Grass	1/2" to 1 1/2"
❑ Improved Bermuda Grass	1/2" to 1"
❑ Bluegrass	1 1/2" to 2"
❑ Centipede Grass	1" to 2"
❑ Fescue Grass	2" to 2 1/2"
❑ Annual Ryegrass	1 1/2" to 2"
❑ St. Augustine Grass	1" to 3"
❑ Zoysia Grass	1/2" to 1 1/2"

Aerating a lawn allows water, air, and fertilizer to more easily penetrate into the root layer. An aerator either pokes holes into the turf or pulls out small cores of grass and soil. You can rent an aerator and do the job yourself.

Gardeners in Walt Disney World Resort aerate some turf areas three times a year with a core aerator. They prefer this type of aerator because the tines move up and down vertically removing the soil core without leaving a hole with compacted sides like the roller-type aerator does.

This nicely manicured lawn fronts Minnie Mouses's House in Disneyland Park.

Proper watering techniques assure good grass color, growth, shoot density, and recuperation from stress regardless of the amount of rainfall. Most Disney turf areas are watered by automatic underground irrigation systems with rotary, oscillating, or fixed spray heads. The amount of water needed varies with grass type, soil type, wind, rain, temperature, the topography or slope, and the amount of use and maintenance the area experiences. Water needs to penetrate the soil a minimum of 6" to be effective. If your grass has a bluish cast to it or footprints remain after you've walked across the lawn, water now!

Most lawns benefit from a fertilizing in spring and in fall with a slow-release fertilizer. Select a complete fertilizer containing nitrogen, phosphorus, and potassium at a rate of 2:1:1 for the spring application and 1:2:2 for the fall application. The warm Florida temperature and year 'round growing season in Walt Disney World Resort sometimes make fertilizing a priority seven times a year. Disney horticulturists prefer a fertilizer high in nitrogen to promote good green color and rapid growth.

A Sod Roof is Tops at Norway in EPCOT

The Norwegian people understand the important balance that should exist between the house and garden. Many gardeners in Norway believe that a home is not finished if both the interior and exterior surroundings are not gracefully designed.

Accordingly, keynotes of simplicity and serenity are often incorporated into their native garden designs. In the picturesque Scandinavian countryside, a traveler could happen upon a sod-covered roof hostel similar to the replica at Norway in EPCOT.

Although few of these cottages now remain in the unspoiled mountain wilderness of Norway, some are still nostalgically maintained and open to accommodate overnight guests.

The zoysia grass turf roof on the Norway cottage requires quite a bit of maintenance and care to retain its natural appearance. There is a submersed irrigation system that runs on a regular schedule and the turf is fertilized two to three times annually to keep it green and growing.

During the summers, Disney horticulturists are busy planting 2" peat-potted wildflowers across the roof to capture the authentic Norwegian country look.

Ground cover is an interesting and practical alternative to grass.

Ground Covers

Incorporating ground covers into your garden design adds an aesthetically pleasing finishing touch to the landscape. The diverse textures and colors introduce abundant visual interest while conveying a unified feeling to the surroundings. Ground covers can also solve many garden dilemmas.

Ground covers are an excellent alternative to grass because they require less water, fertilizing, and maintenance, and have very few pest and disease foes. They are planted on slopes where erosion is a problem and under shady trees and shrubs where it's a struggle for grass to grow. Many gardeners add ground covers to areas that are difficult to mow, such as rock gardens, among stepping stones, on hills, and along stairs and foundations. Certain ground covers are planted in place of mulch as a weed control. Walking on ground covers should be avoided, and usually is, so they can be planted to divert foot traffic around a certain area. Some herbs, like rosemary, mint, and creeping thyme, are used as practical, attractive, and tasty ground covers. Wild strawberry plants spread and form a dense cover of green leaves, delicate flowers, and colorful fruit.

Sometimes ground covers are planted in specific designs in parterre-like fashion. For example, dark green Irish moss and lighter green Scotch moss is planted in Storybook Land in Disneyland Park creating a wonderful patchwork effect near the fairy-tale windmills.

Maintenance requirements for ground covers are similar to those for flowers. Most prefer rich soil, although certain plants, like ajuga, will grow under just about any condition. Space each plant depending upon its growth habit and recommendations on the plant tag or offered by nursery staff. Once established, many plants multiply by themselves and most others can be propagated by root division, layering, or cutting.

Common Ground Covers

African Daisy
Ajuga
Armeria maritima

Artemisia
Asiatic Jasmine
Campanula
Candytuft
Chamomile
Creeping Juniper
Creeping Mint
Creeping Phlox

Cotoneaster
Crown Vetch
Fern
Gazania
Heather
Hosta
Indian Strawberry
Irish Moss
Lamb's-ear
Lantana
Lily-of-the-Valley
Lilyturf
Lippia Grass
(not a true grass)
Mondo Grass
Moneywort
Pachysandra
Periwinkle
Pink

Scotch Moss
Sedum
Snow-in-Summer
Spreading Yew
Star Jasmine
Sweet Woodruff
Thyme

Vines

Few sights are as breathtaking as a shaded arbor of lavender wisteria, or a blanket of scarlet-hued bougainvillea sprawling over a stucco wall, or a trellis covered with a cascade of morning glory. Vines are as versatile as they are plentiful. Some are annuals and others are perennials. They can thrive in containers, create curtains of color on fences, pergolas, or walls, magnificently frame a garden gate, fill the air with heavenly fragrance, or conceal a less-than-pleasing view.

The flowers on many vines, like trumpet vine for example, are remarkably enticing to hummingbirds. A wall of leafy, green perennial vines provides a wonderful background "canvas" for flowers or a shady respite on a sunny afternoon if positioned just right. From verdant green to all the colors in your imagination, vines are an important element in any gardener's palette.

Many vines can be trained to follow specific shapes with some skillful pruning and by planting at the foot of a fence, wire frame, lattice screen, or rows of string or wire. Vines climb in several different ways: tendrils that spiral around the support; twining stems, or disc-shaped suckers or rootlets that attach themselves to a surface. Other vines will ramble aimlessly unless you provide support for them.

Vines adorn an Adventureland restaurant sign in Magic Kingdom Park.

Vines form a natural frame in Disney's Caribbean Beach Resort.

You can use twine, paper-covered wire, wide rubber bands, plastic ties, or raffia on light-weight vines. Remember that eventually these will break down and need to be replaced. For heavy vines, especially some perennials, you might try cotton or plastic clothesline, strips of canvas fabric, heavy-duty insulated wire, or rubber tree ties. Toggle bolts, eye bolts, special staples, u-bolts, molly bolts, and concrete nails are some of the hardware used to attach vines to wood, plaster, and masonry surfaces.

Perennial vines are usually purchased from the nursery or catalog or may be started as transplants or cuttings. Be sure the vine you purchase or start yourself is appropriate to your climate because wintry winds and dipping temperatures can cause great damage to many of these climbing beauties.

Annual vines grow more rapidly than perennial vines as they only have a short time to put on their show. You can buy annual vine seeds and start your own or purchase transplants for quicker results.

A tangle of vines forms a dense blanket at Critter Country in Disneyland Park.

Perennial vines typically require pruning to keep them blossoming and in control from taking over the surroundings. Annual vines usually don't need pruning, but do benefit from having their stems rearranged once in a while. Water and fertilize your vines according to their cultural requirements and you'll soon be the envy of the neighborhood.

Common Vines

Boston Ivy
Bougainvillea
Cardinal Climber
English Ivy
Five-leaf Akebia
Grape

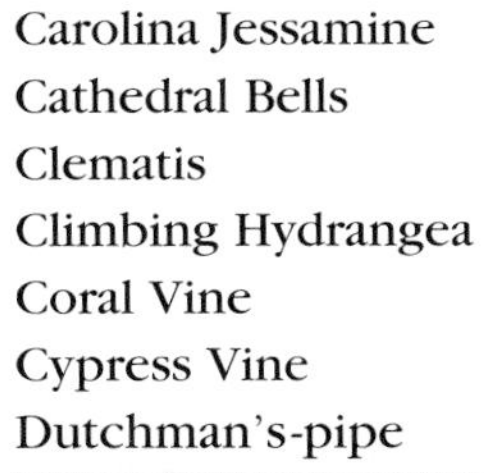

Carolina Jessamine
Cathedral Bells
Clematis
Climbing Hydrangea
Coral Vine
Cypress Vine
Dutchman's-pipe
Honeysuckle
Jasmine
Mandevilla
Moonflower
Morning Glory
Nasturtium
Passionflower

Silver-lace
Trumpet Vine
Virginia Creeper
Winter Creeper
Wisteria

TRIVIA

- There are over 11,000 interior landscape plants, 10,100 rose bushes, 100,000 trees, and more than one million permanent shrubs at home in Walt Disney World Resort.

- Landscaping in the 30,000 acre Walt Disney World Resort ranges from the exotic jungles of Adventureland to the deserts of Frontierland in Magic Kingdom Park, to the glamour of a palm-lined boulevard in Disney-MGM Studios Theme Park.

- When the Interstate 5 Freeway was under construction in southern California in the 1950s, Disneyland Park had nursery contractors procure many large trees that would have otherwise been destroyed.

- Bill Evans, the primary landscape contractor for the original Disneyland Park landscape installation, used a WWII weapons carrier (truck) to transport many of the trees once they reached the Disneyland Park site. The old truck continued to act as the Landscape Department's workhorse up until the 1980s. It was formally retired in 1993 and now rests proudly at the backstage nursery in Disneyland Park.

- Approximately 1,700 plant species are represented in flora gathered from all over the U.S. and 50 foreign nations at the Walt Disney World Resort.

- The large grouping of Senegal date palms growing in Tomorrowland in Disneyland Park was dug up and transported there in the 1950s from the Hollywood home of movie mogul Cecil B. DeMille.

- The Walt Disney World Resort Nursery is responsible for some 20,000 field-grown trees. An average of 900 specimen trees are moved from the Nursery to help create "instant landscapes" across the property each year.

- Walt Disney World Resort is home to a collection of over 800 exquisite and exotic orchids.

Flower Gardens

This hillside garden in Disneyland Park is a sprin time bouquet color.

It's hard to resist the temptation to pause and admire a spectacular flower garden. Imagine the rich tapestry of color, the diversity of textures, the soft fragrances, and the sight and sound of leaves swaying in the wind.

Asters follow the curving wall fronting China in EPCOT.

A garden blooming from spring through the first frost, or even throughout the entire year, doesn't happen by chance. It takes clever planning, patient experimentation, and practice to coax the plants into blooming at the right time and place in your garden.

Many people consider their gardens as ever-changing works in progress. They stand by their favorite perennials, try recommended cultivars, intersperse popular annuals or delicate wildflowers, and plant a variety of bulbs. Distinctive foliage plants provide interesting backgrounds, pull the whole display together, and furnish a screen for fading perennial and bulb leaves.

Throughout the year, Disney gardeners test over 500 plant varieties in "bedding plant trials" to determine what plants will work best for them. The results are published each winter and summer and used in planning their gardens. A computer database keeps track of bedding plant schedules. The versatile program also includes such features as flowerbed theme guidelines and "look up" tables for plant identification.

A stone border neatly corrals a colorful medley of flowers.

Selecting Plants and Planning Ahead

Home gardeners don't need a computer database or program to have a beautiful garden. Simple programs are available now, but a pad of paper and a pencil should suffice for most flower garden planning, whether you're starting from seed, buying bedding plants, or planting bulbs.

The most practical and cost-effective way to plan a successful garden is to select the appropriate plants for the season, site location, soil type, and the design requirements you have in mind.

The "seasonality" of bedding plants is a major consideration for Disney gardeners when making their flower selections. The term "seasonality" refers to identifying the season or seasons of peak performance for particular plants. Tried-and-true plant cultivars (plant varieties grown with specific characteristics) also get their stamp of approval. Matching plants to the best season for growth and planting cultivars suggested for your climate zone are sure-fire ways to enjoy gorgeous garden color.

Make believe you're planning a rectangular flower garden to be located against a wall of your home. You would select some of your plants based on the season. Then certain plants

Ranunculas cut a pretty path in the Victoria Garden in EPCOT.

would be picked based on the soil type and whether the garden was located in sun or shade or in a wet or dry spot. Plant height and finishing-off size (a plant's maximum height) would also need to be considered. Low plants would obviously be planted in front while medium- and tall-sized plants would be added in the background.

Blossom color and bloom time are also very important. Some perennials and bulbs only produce a showy bloom for a short time, then become dormant. Strategically interplanting annuals, biennials, and distinctive foliage plants among the perennials and bulbs will ensure a constant supply of color.

Remember, too, that you'll have to maintain the garden. You would select plants requiring less maintenance if you have little time to spare. A garden planted against a wall can only be weeded and maintained from the front and sides if you don't leave a path for yourself between the last row of plants and the wall. Leave enough space so you can get to the back without crushing tender stalks.

Tall, densely growing flowers can form an impressive hedge.

The complementary foliage and flower colors of caladium and salvia are a delight to the eye.

Make a daily or weekly journal of your successes and failures for future reference. Many bookstores carry beautiful gardener's journals, complete with spaces for photos, gardening tips, and interesting quotations about gardening. You might note what plants did well, what pest problems you encountered, when blossoms made their first appearance, how long the blooms lasted, and any other information you feel would help you plan for the next season or year. As time passes, you'll know almost intuitively what to plant, where to plant it, and when it will bloom.

Tips for Flower Garden Selections

- ❑ The size of the garden is not important. Begin with a small 4'-square plot and make a plan to add to it.
- ❑ Seed catalogs are a great source of information about bedding plant varieties and will give you cultural requirements for the flowers you are considering.
- ❑ Avoid "fire sales" (e.g., pansy clearances at the end of pansy season — May in most places), they may not be the deal you thought they were.
- ❑ Give consideration to garden site characteristics such as light intensity, soil type, irrigation, drainage, and display objective.
- ❑ When planning your flower garden, ponder formal vs. informal flowerbeds, mass plantings vs. flower mix, color scheme, fragrance, texture, flower shape, and plant height.
- ❑ Select proven varieties such as the All-American Selection winners for vigorous plants. Look at plant catalogs to find out which plants are AAS-designated.
- ❑ Pick deep green healthy plants and check them for pests before you bring them home.
- ❑ Buy plants that are in bloom and bud. Flowering plants should be just beginning to go into bloom for a continuing show of color.

Twilight descends on Morocco in EPCOT, intensifying the colors of these New Guinea impatiens.

- ❑ If grooming time is a concern, try low-maintenance, self-cleaning annuals like wax begonia and impatiens.

Imaginative Flower Gardens

Disney gardeners plant their flowerbeds in many different configurations, using a multitude of plants, to enhance a location, reinforce a particular theme, or just beautify the landscape.

Peachy-pink geraniums furnish old-fashioned appeal.

You can create a solid band of uniform height and bold color by planting just one type of flower in volume. Impatiens, chrysanthemum, poinsettia, and salvia are good candidates. Planting rows of colorful plants side by side creates a wonderful rainbow effect.

An upsweep of color is produced by planting very low plants in front, followed by taller and taller plants in the background. Disney gardeners also plant plants of two or more different genus' together, like crossandra and salvia, for a "salt and pepper" effect. A mix of plant types, heights, and colors creates an old-fashioned, cottage garden look.

Ageratum, wax begonias, and marigolds compose a living rainbow.

Create a circular flower garden around a tree. Follow the curves of a brick path leading to your garage. Plant a bed in front of a line of bushes. Try a raised bed of flowers if you have back trouble or other physical limitations. Plant along your driveway

or a fence. Add a flower garden to a child's playhouse. Plant flowers to cut for floral arrangements, dry for everlasting bouquets, or to make potpourri. Attract butterflies and hummingbirds by planting flowers they love.

Use your imagination when designing your flower garden and review gardening magazines and books for ideas. Inspiration can also come from some surprising places — a fabric pattern, the shape of the garden hose lying on the ground, a magazine ad, a greeting card, or an old oil painting. Keep your eyes and mind open!

Easy-care wax begonias encircle the base of a tree.

***Butterflies** are captivated by a variety of flowers.*

Mickey's "Best Bets" for Flower Gardening

Easy-to-grow Favorites

Alyssum
Aster

Celosia
Chrysanthemum
Cyclamen

Daffodil
Dahlia
Dianthus
Geranium
Gerbera Daisy
Hollyhock

Impatiens
Marigold
Melanpodium
Pansy
Penstemon
Petunia
Poinsettia
Ranunculus
Salvia

Snapdragon
Tulip
Viola
Wax Begonia
Zinnia

How to Prepare a Flower Bed

What You'll Need

- ❑ Soil pH test kit
- ❑ Soil amendments like decomposed pine bark, coarse sand, wood chips, and peat moss
- ❑ Cultivator, rototiller, or shovel
- ❑ Grading rake
- ❑ High nitrogen granular fertilizer with micronutrients

A mass planting of chrysanthemums creates a bold carpet of color.

1. Evaluate the soil pH. A pH of approximately 6.0 is desirable.

2. Remove all plant debris such as root balls, dead leaves, twigs, and weeds with the grading rake.

3. Mix the soil with peat, sand, decomposed pine bark, and wood chips to enrich the soil and improve drainage and moisture retention. Disney gardeners in Florida find a ratio of 40% peat moss, to 40% coarse sand, to 10% decomposed pine bark, to 10% wood chips an excellent annual soil mix. In Disneyland Park, gardeners use less sand because the Park is built on an old riverbed and already has plenty of coarse sand. Nitrolized redwood and leaf mulch is the higher percentage in their soil mix.

4. Top dress with the granular fertilizer per package directions and then till the soil with the cultivator, rototiller, or shovel to a depth of 6".

5. Grade the bed level with the grading rake to the desired level and you're ready for planting.

Spacing Your Flowers

All plants have optimum spacing requirements. Proper spacing of your plants is important for air circulation (to avoid disease problems) and allows the plants to grow in a natural shape. It also prevents certain taller plants from looming over smaller ones and lets the plants be seen at their best advantage. A garden should look full, but not crowded. Plants not only grow taller, many spread out sideways. Overcrowded plants start fighting over light, water, and nutrients, too.

Properly spaced flowers grow in a natural profusion.

Flower Gardens

Spacing for Selected Flowers

❑ Ageratum	10"
❑ Begonia	8-11"
❑ Celosia cristata	8-11"
❑ Celosia plumosa	8"
❑ Chrysanthemum	8-12"
❑ Gerbera Daisy	12-14"
❑ Impatiens	12"
❑ Marigold	8-12"
❑ Pansy	6-8"
❑ Petunia	10-14"
❑ Rudebeckia	12"

Planting Bedding Plants

Water your bedding plants in their containers before planting if they are dry to avoid damaging the tender roots. If a plant is tightly rooted in the container, gently loosen it (soil and all) from the container. Handle the plant by the soil ball and avoid handling the stem as much as possible. Lightly score the roots with a knife, being careful not to remove any soil.

Start by planting from the outer edge of the bed in towards the back or center of the bed as per your predetermined design and plant spacing requirements. If you run out of plants, you can hide the gaps in the back and fill in the spaces later.

When digging a hole, make the hole larger than the root ball by inserting the trowel into the soil and pulling back on the trowel. Carefully set the plant into the hole — avoiding any abrupt motion that would break the stem. The top of the root ball should be even with ground level. Set some annuals, such as pansy and Gerbera daisy, a little higher than grade. Gently firm and level the soil around the original root ball making sure that the plant is standing straight.

Gently water each plant immediately after planting using a water breaker. Follow-up with individual plant watering in addition to the regular irrigation schedule for rootbound flowers or plants that send out roots too slowly. For instance, Gerbera daisies need individual watering for up to two weeks after planting. Make a final top dressing of fertilizer at the end of planting using the same rate as when preparing the flowerbed.

Maintenance

This "wild" flower collection in Disney's Wilderness Lodge is low-maintenance, sun- and drought-tolerant.

Once planted, proper maintenance will keep your flower garden looking good throughout the seasons. Depending upon the varieties chosen, properly maintained annual beds will last from three to six months.

Disney gardeners apply a liquid fertilizer regularly to keep their plants growing, healthy, and in constant bloom. Water as necessary, and remember that wilting doesn't always mean the plants need more water. It could be a problem (like root rot) that warrants a closer inspection and treatment. Some plants, like hollyhock, should never be watered from above because wet leaves encourage and make them more susceptible to disease spread.

Cultivate around the flowers to aerate the soil and prevent the germination of weed seeds. Pull new weeds immediately. They not only detract from the beauty of the flower beds, they steal precious water and nutrients. Remove annuals when they are past their prime and replant with new annuals for a fresh look.

Prolong the blooms and extend the life of the flowers by pinching off dead flowers (deadheading). Deadheading also prevents plants from going to seed too soon and triggers new side growth and budding, resulting in bushier plants with more blossoms. Disneyland gardeners extend the life of penstemon, snapdragon, and delphinium up to an additional two months by deadheading.

Check weekly for pests or diseases and treat them quickly. Try the least toxic treatment first, and spot treat rather than mass spray, if using chemical controls.

Common Bedding Plants

Ageratum
Aster
Balsam
Begonia
Bells of Ireland
Browallia

Calendula
California Poppy
Candytuft
Celosia
Cleome
Coleus
Cosmos

Dahlia
Dusty Miller
Euphorbia
Gazania
Gomphrena
Hollyhock
Impatiens
Larkspur
Lobelia
Marigold
Morning Glory

Nasturtium
Nicotiana
Pansy
Petunia
Phlox
Poppy
Salvia
Sweet Alyssum
Sunflower

Common Perennials

Alcea
Armeria
Aster
Astilbe
Bergenia

Campanula
Candytuft
Carnation
(annual in some places)
Chrysanthemum

Clematis
Columbine
Coreopsis
Daylily
Delphinium
Dianthus
(annual in some places)
Digitalis
Echinacea
Gaillardia
Geranium
(annual in some places)
Goldenrod
Globethistle
Gypsophilia
Helianthus
Helleborus
Hosta
Jacob's Ladder
Lady's Mantle
Liatris
Lunaria
Lungwort
Lupine

Peony
Periwinkle
Phlox
Poppy
Primrose
Rudebeckia
Salvia
Sedum
Trillium
Verbena
Viola
Violet
Yucca

Common Bulbs

Agapanthus
Allium
Amaryllis
Anemone

Caladium
Calla Lily
Canna
Chionodoxa
Crocus
Cyclamen
Daffodil
Dahlia
Freesia
Gladiolus
Grape Hyacinth
Hyacinth
Iris
Lily of the Valley
Narcissus
Tulip

TRIVIA

- The largest annual display area is at Canada in EPCOT. For the Fall Mum Show, over 17,000 mums in various colors take 200 hours to plant in the Victoria Garden.

- Walt Disney Theme Parks and Resorts glow with winter colors and holiday decorations from the last week of November until the first of the year. In Walt Disney World Resort, 60,000 poinsettias greet visitors and at Disneyland Park and The Disneyland Hotel, 25,000 of the colorful plants enhance the festive spirit.

- Black pansy, iresine (blood plant), black mondo grass, and Medusa's head (euphorbia) are some of the themed plants adding to the spooky atmosphere in front of The Haunted Mansion in Disneyland Park.

- At Walt Disney World Resort, 30% of each landscape dollar goes to the purchase, installation, and maintenance of bedding plants.

- One thousand tulips and 500 daffodils are planted on Matterhorn Mountain in Disneyland Park.

- More than 2,000,000 annuals are planted each year to add that "splash" of color to Walt Disney World Resort.

The simple, unsurpassed beauty of the rose has enchanted us throughout history.

The delicate, fragrant rose. The Queen of Flowers. Throughout time, roses have been lovingly immortalized in paintings, poems, photographs, sculptures, and songs, touching our lives in countless ways we don't even realize. Shakespeare even wrote, "Of all the flowers, methinks a rose is best." Our enchantment with the rose has extended through the centuries. There was a time when wealthy Romans slumbered on plump cushions of rose petals, draped their cups and tables with garlands of roses, dined on delicacies featuring rose petals, and bathed in fountains of gushing rose-scented water. It's even rumored Nero spent what would now amount to $100,000 on roses for just one special evening. And if that doesn't seem decadent enough, Cleopatra's floors were reportedly strewn with an 18"-thick carpet of the velvety petals.

The likeness of a rose appropriately adorns this sign in Disneyland Park*.*

Venus, the mythological Goddess of Love, is said to have been the inspiration for the creation of the rose. According to legend, the Earth was so envious of her extraordinary beauty it vowed to create something of parallel perfection. After some deliberation, the Earth combined the most heavenly fragrance and the most exquisite form to create the rose. Other legends attribute the rose with strange, magical powers usually relating to affairs of the heart.

Many brides have walked down rose petal-strewn paths on their wedding days, carrying bountiful bouquets of sweet-smelling roses. On Valentine's Day, anniversaries, birthdays, and

The Roses of Walt Disney Theme Parks and Resorts

Impressive rose displays can be found throughout the Walt Disney Theme Parks and Resorts. For example, more than 10,000 rose bushes in over 40 varieties are used to enhance the theme and architectural style of certain areas in Walt Disney World Resort. Elegant tree roses are planted near ticket gates and entrances to soften the hard, geometric edges of railings and bush roses accentuate the Victorian theme of the Main Street Town Square. Miniature roses add a touch of charm to the formal British gardens of United Kingdom in EPCOT and a captivating All-America Rose Selection Display Garden holds court just outside Cinderella Castle.

In Disneyland Park, hundreds of award-winning pink, lavender, and magenta floribunda roses are planted at the entrance as a colorful welcome for guests. Lovely polyantha roses bloom near the water's edge in Snow White's Grotto, enhancing the whimsical, fairy-tale setting. In New Orleans Square, pink and red flowering roses highlight the Mardi Gras atmosphere.

other special occasions, roses are often given as romantic tokens of love. Some people believe the simple gesture of presenting a single rose is more poignant than bestowing a full dozen.

In 1935, a rose and jasmine-based perfume, touted as "the world's costliest perfume," made its debut. It still reigns as a classic favorite today. One reason the perfume is so expensive is because it takes an incredible 180 pounds of rose petals to make just one ounce of rose oil!

Rose patterns have appeared on tableware, fabrics, greeting cards, wallpapers, stamps, emblems, awards, currency, and even in candy form. Many proud parents name newborn girls Rose, Rosa, and other variations, in honor of the dainty flower. The bewitching allure of the rose is enduring and powerful.

Types of Roses

There are several categories of roses, including old garden (or antique), hybrid tea, floribunda, grandiflora, polyantha, shrub, climbing, miniature, and tree roses. Each type has its own special charm and appeal for the garden. There are also rose varieties within these categories that are bred for specific climatic conditions. Some of these cultivars are very cold hardy to endure freezes and others are more tolerant to heat and humidity.

Old Garden Roses

Old garden roses are defined as those roses whose class predates the hybrid tea rose's introduction in 1867. Many people have a love for the nostalgic and historic aspect of these roses and set aside special places in their landscape just for these "antiques." Old roses are also very hardy in the winter, easy to care for, live a long time, and have their own unique fragrances, forms, and beauty.

Common Old Garden Roses

- ❑ Alba (grows dense, tall, blooms once per year, disease-resistant)
- ❑ Bourbon (beautiful double repeat blooms, fragrant, blooms repeatedly)
- ❑ Centifolia (also Cabbage or Provence roses; each bloom has over 100 fragrant petals, blooms once per year)
- ❑ China (delicate, tender, blooms repeatedly)
- ❑ Damask (very fragrant, most bloom only once per year)
- ❑ Gallacia (the oldest rose known, blooms once per year)
- ❑ Hybrid Perpetual (blooms repeatedly, hardy)
- ❑ Noisette (climbs in mild areas, fragrant, blooms all summer)
- ❑ Species Roses (hardy, some bloom only once, others bloom repeatedly)

Modern Roses

In 1867, the first "modern" rose was accidentally created. A fluke crossing of a hybrid perpetual with a tea rose produced a rose called 'La France.' This new rose, classified as a hybrid tea, had the characteristics of both the parent plants. It bloomed often and had neat growth habits like the tea rose and was hardy in the winter like the perpetual rose. This success spurred a flurry of hybridizing and experimentation which continues today.

Hybrid Tea

Hybrid tea roses scent a room with delightful fragrance and typify the classic style of today's roses. Swirling petals bloom in nearly every color but blue on plants that grow 2' to 5' tall. Their long stems make them perfect for vases and floral arrangements.

Hybrid Tea

Floribunda

Floribunda

The name itself implies many flowers and that's exactly what makes this beautiful rose so popular. The floribundas bloom profusely on long stems in a huge variety of colors, forms, and sizes. They are a wonderful landscape rose because they are quite hardy, compact, disease-resistant, and have a dense growing habit. Many people use them as hedges and borders or as dramatic mass plantings.

Grandiflora

In 1954, the grandiflora class was developed for the 'Queen Elizabeth' rose, a cross between the hybrid tea and floribunda. These tall roses are often used as a background or screen behind other, lower-growing plants. They are very hardy, flower continuously, and are often used in floral arrangements.

Grandiflora

Polyantha

Polyantha

Around the same time the hybrid tea made its auspicious debut, the polyantha class was created. These roses usually bloom with clusters of unique, cup-shaped blossoms, low to the ground, and in lovely shades of pink, red, and orange.

Shrub Rose

Shrub Roses

Shrub roses come in all heights from low-growing ground covers to tall sizes for hedges and background plantings. They are disease-resistant, bloom for long periods, and are easy to maintain.

Climbing Roses

Climbing roses are considered by some to be the most beautiful of all the roses. Spilling opulently over trellises, arbors, fences, and walls, they create a soft, romantic, old-fashioned scenario anyone would stop and admire. With a little support, these long-caned beauties can grow to incredible heights and lengths, producing abundant clusters of fragrant flowers.

Climbing Rose

Miniature roses are in perfect proportion to Mickey's Starland in the Magic Kingdom Park.

Miniature Roses

Miniature roses are tiny replicas of their big sisters in every way. Their minute stems, leaves, and blossoms grow to heights reaching from only a few inches to a demure 1½'. Some blossoms resemble miniature hybrid tea roses and others look like peewee-sized floribundas. Their compact growing habits make them perfect for containers, small hedges, and as accent plantings.

Tree Roses

Tree roses really capture your attention and imagination with their elegant stems and lushly growing heads. Professional growers create them by carefully grafting any type of rose on top of a stem. Usually a stake is secured to the stem to ensure straight and sturdy growth. Many people pot tree roses in containers and use them as an eye-catching accent near a front door, or in the patio or pool area. In a flower bed, surrounded by annuals and perennials, the tree rose becomes a real garden focal point. Many tree roses spread and flower profusely, and some even have a "weeping" shape. Tree roses are usually quite tender and can be damaged by cold temperatures. Be sure to wrap them in burlap, bury the canes in the ground, or bring them inside when you're expecting temperatures below freezing.

A tree rose grows tall at Disney's Yacht and Beach Club Resorts.

Selecting Your Roses

The astounding variety of roses may cause you some pleasant confusion when it comes time to make your selections. Begin by evaluating your yard and determine what function you want the roses to perform. Do you want roses for cutting and bringing indoors? Do you need to cleverly conceal an eyesore? Do you want to create a colorful border? Do you want a relaxing place to stop and smell the roses? Are you considering using roses as accents? Or are you just fascinated by miniature flowers?

At the plant nursery you'll notice most of the roses are sporting rather detailed tags listing their type, name, color, growth habits, and planting information. The better roses are classified as superior by either the All-America Rose Selections (AARS) or The American Rose Society (ARS). If possible, select these roses.

The AARS is a national organization of professional growers who test and rate new varieties of roses based on foliage, flower form, bloom frequency, substance, color, habit, vigor, disease resistance, hardiness, fragrance, and novelty. The plants with the highest ratings receive the prestigious AARS award.

The ARS is a group of amateur and professional growers nationwide, who categorize all roses into 17 color classifications ranging from white to russet. Every three years the members are surveyed to establish rose ratings. A 10-point scale is used, with a score of 10 given to a "perfect" rose.

There are many local and regional rose societies and clubs, as well as public rose gardens, throughout the country. If you're serious about your rose gardening, they're worth visiting or joining.

Selecting and Preparing the Planting Location

Roses need six to eight hours of direct sun (preferably) or partial shade each day. Morning sun is the best because it quickly dries the morning dew from the plants, reducing the risk of diseases. If you live in a zone where the summers are very hot, select a site with some light afternoon shade. Roses also don't like wet feet, so select a site with good drainage. Be sure to select a location where the roses can live indefinitely, away from competing trees and shrubs. Roses usually like to be protected from the wind by a fence, hedge, or other barrier.

Once you've selected your location, cover the area with 2" of peat moss. For every 10 square feet of planting area, add 4 oz. of 12-4-8 fertilizer and a liberal amount of composted cow manure. Thoroughly mix the soil and amendments, then turn the soil over to a depth of 18" with a shovel.

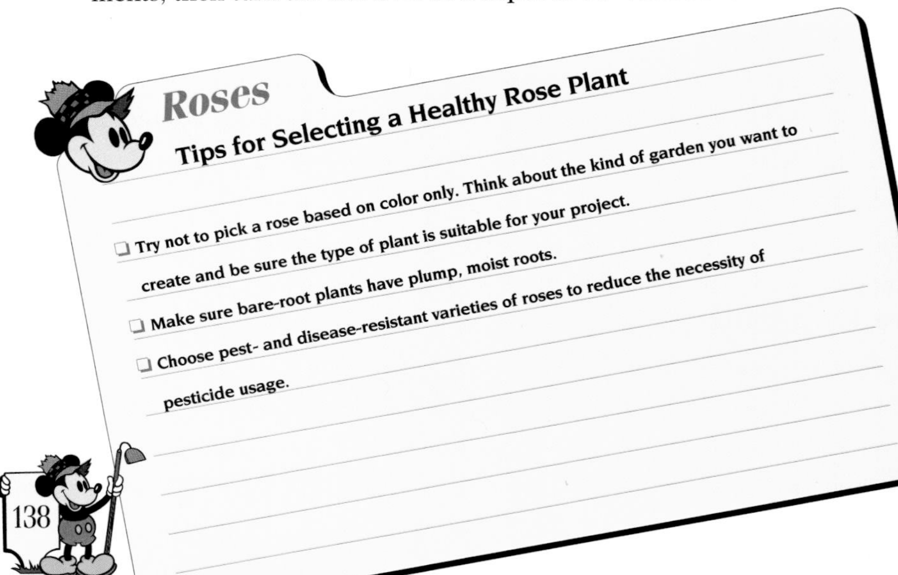

Roses

Tips for Selecting a Healthy Rose Plant

- ❑ Try not to pick a rose based on color only. Think about the kind of garden you want to create and be sure the type of plant is suitable for your project.
- ❑ Make sure bare-root plants have plump, moist roots.
- ❑ Choose pest- and disease-resistant varieties of roses to reduce the necessity of pesticide usage.

Spacing

Most roses, like hybrid tea, grandiflora, and floribunda, are usually planted 2' to 4' apart, but certain types require more or less space. Shrub and old garden roses grow large and need to be planted 4' to 6' apart. Climbing roses are trained horizontally and should be planted 8' to 10' apart. Miniature roses only need spacing of 8" to 18" depending upon their size at maturity.

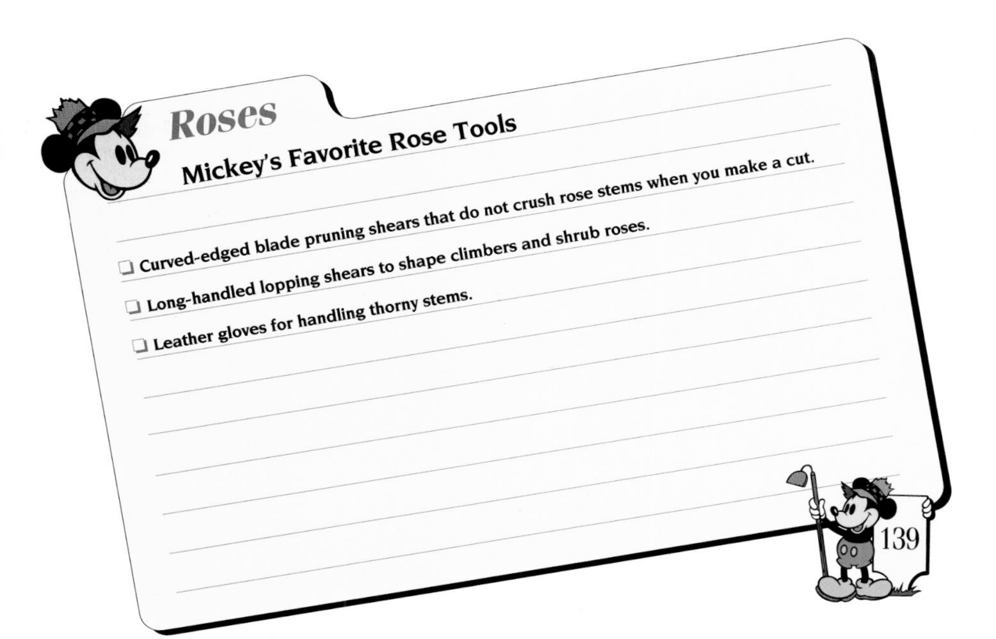

How to Plant Bare-root Roses

What You'll Need

- ❑ Tub filled with water for soaking
- ❑ Digging shovel
- ❑ One quart compost, peat moss, or other organic matter
- ❑ Rose pruners
- ❑ One bare-root rose plant
- ❑ Hose and water breaker

1. Soak the roots overnight before planting.

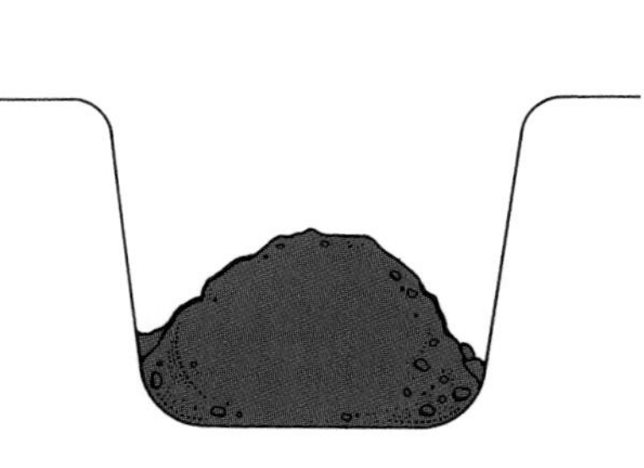

2. Choose a deeply spaded, prepared bed in a well-drained area. Dig a hole 18" wide by 18" deep. Add your organic matter, mixing well with the soil. Form a cone-shaped pile of this mixture in the planting hole. Pack the mound firmly.

3 Gently prune branches to within 12" of the grafting point. Remove any broken or injured roots or canes thinner than a pencil. Place the rose on the soil cone so the bud union (the swelling at the base of the stem) is just below ground level after the ground settles. Spread the roots out and down the soil mound, working soil around the roots to eliminate any air pockets. Firm the soil around the roots and add more soil until the hole is three-quarters full.

4 Mound up the leftover soil to form a dam-like water basin around the rose. Water immediately, then wait until the soil is almost drained before watering again.

5 Do not fertilize until the first new leaves appear, then use a fertilizer that has a balance of fast-acting plant food or a commercial rose fertilizer.

Roses

Tips for Planting Bare-root Roses

- Bare-root roses, as the name implies, are sold without any soil around the roots. It is best to plant them during their dormant period and after the ground has thawed, usually in late winter or early spring.
- You can plant roses in the fall if you live in a climate where winter temperatures do not dip below zero, but be sure to add some mulch for extra protection.
- Plant bare-root roses as soon as possible once you get them home. Store them in a cool, dark place if you can't plant them for a few days and keep the roots moist with either packing material, sawdust, damp newspaper, or damp peat moss.

How to Plant Container Roses

What You'll Need

- ❑ Digging shovel
- ❑ One container-grown rose plant
- ❑ Hose and water breaker

1 Dig a hole twice the width of the containe Gently remove the rose from its container being careful not to damage the roots.

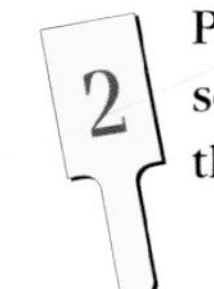

2 Place the plant in the hole so that once th soil is leveled, the graft union is ½" below the soil surface.

3 Fill the hoie up with the remaining soil, packing it firmly. Mound up leftover soil to form a dam-like water basin around the rose. Water immediately, then wait until the soil is almost drained before watering again.

4 Do not fertilize until the first leaves appear, then use a fertilizer that has a balance of fast-acting plant food or a commercial rose fertilizer.

Roses

Tips for Planting Container-grown Roses

- You can extend the planting season into summer by purchasing container-grown roses.
- Always remove the plants from plastic, metal, and compressed-fiber or cardboard containers before planting. However, if the rose is in full leaf or flower and is planted in a compressed-fiber or cardboard container, just remove the bottom of the container and cut slits into the sides to ensure unrestricted root growth.

Watering

Correct watering techniques will improve plant growth, and produce bigger, more colorful and abundant blooms. If you choose to water by overhead sprinkling, either with a hose-end sprayer or a watering can, be sure to do the watering in the morning so the plant leaves have time to dry before sunset. Remember, though, overhead watering will rinse off any preventive sprays or dusts you may have applied.

Many people have soaker hoses or drip irrigation systems permanently installed in their gardens. This method of watering uses less water than overhead sprinkling and keeps the water off the foliage.

A good rule of thumb for watering roses is, "1" of water per week." If you give the plants one good soaking a week (vs. several light waterings) you'll encourage deeper roots, which lead to stronger plants. However, if your soil is sandy, or you live in a particularly warm or windy area, you will have to water more often.

Fertilizing

Once the new growth is well under way, apply a commercial rose fertilizer or fertilizer such as 5-10-5, according to package directions. Roses are usually fed at least three times a year. The first time is immediately after pruning, the next is directly after the first bloom cycle, and finally, two months before the first frost of fall.

If you want larger flowers, fertilize once a month during the growing season. Apply the fertilizers evenly over the pre-moistened soil surface and work into the soil gently with a hand-held cultivator. Water well. You will have to fertilize every two weeks if you are using a liquid fertilizer because this type leaches from the soil very quickly.

Pruning

Pruning roses is the most important step of proper rose care. Careful pruning ensures large, healthy plants, and encourages basal breaks (new canes) to grow from the bottoms of the roses. The basal breaks allow the plants to regenerate themselves each year. Pruning can also help prevent disease. For example, black spot, a common problem with roses, can survive through the winter on the rose canes. By carefully pruning the roses you can literally "cut away" the problem.

How to Prune Roses

What You'll Need

- ❑ Rose pruners
- ❑ Orange shellac or pruning compound
- ❑ Leather work gloves

1. Cut all dead or diseased canes down to the graft union.

2. Prune any broken, wounded, or canker-covered branches to just below the damage.

3. Trim out any canes that are thinner than a pencil. (Obviously this doesn't apply to miniatures.) Also remove any canes that criss-cross to prevent disease and maintain proper air circulation.

4. Prune all remaining canes to the bud union except for three or four of the newest and strongest canes.

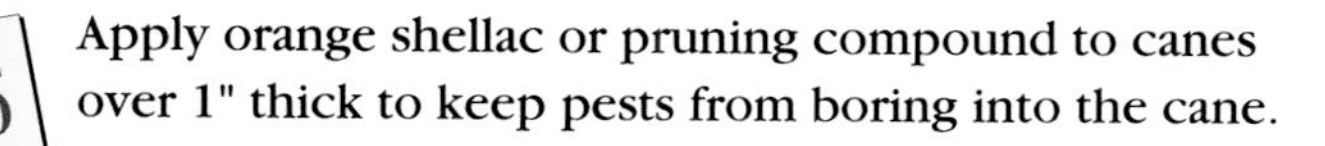

5. Apply orange shellac or pruning compound to canes over 1" thick to keep pests from boring into the cane.

How to Prune Climbing Roses

What You'll Need

❑ Rose pruners
❑ Long-handled lopping shears
❑ Leather work gloves

1 Climbing roses bloom on "old wood" (canes that grew the past year), so prune only to shape and tame dense growth or trim back canes that have grown too long. Cut out any dead, diseased, or wounded canes.

2 Once the plant has finished blooming, prune one or two old canes down to the graft union to allow for growth of new canes.

3 Secure canes to a support like a trellis, fence, wall, or arbor to direct the plant's growth.

Tips for Pruning Roses

- ❑ Walt Disney World gardeners in Florida heavily prune roses — removing three-quarters of the stem — seven weeks prior to Easter, guaranteeing a spring rose show. In autumn the same process is repeated for a splendid rose display at Thanksgiving.
- ❑ In Disneyland Park, roses are pruned heavily in mid-January and again more lightly in fall to prolong blooms through Christmas.
- ❑ Gardeners in other parts of the country should prune established roses when the buds begin to swell.
- ❑ Make cuts at a 45-degree angle about ¼" above the nearest bud that faces out. Don't cut any closer to the bud or you may kill or injure it and conversely, don't cut too high above the bud or the cane may die back. Also, be sure to slant the cut downward, away from the bud, so water runs off properly.
- ❑ Prune newly planted roses lightly the first couple years until they have established a strong set of canes.
- ❑ Always prune blossoms before they go to seed.
- ❑ Remove faded flowers immediately to encourage new growth and quicker reblooming.
- ❑ Cut flowers with a long stem leaving only two or three leaves close to the old wood early in the summer. As the season progress, cut the flowers with a shorter and shorter stem.
- ❑ Watch for suckers that can divert the plant's growth by sapping energy and remove them immediately. Suckers are rose canes that grow with distinctive-looking foliage from the understock beneath the graft unions.
- ❑ Different rose types should be pruned to different heights. Check with your local nursery or garden center for advice.
- ❑ When pruning, clean up all cuttings and fallen plant leaves since these can harbor insects and breed disease.

Disease and Pest Control

There are two main types of parasites that attack roses: fungus, like black spot and mildew, and insects, such as aphids and mites. It's better to prevent a problem than it is to cure it, so don't wait for signs of disease before you start the attack. You can easily control these problems by applying insecticide/fungicide products at regular intervals to the leaves, including the undersides, every two to three weeks. This should take care of most disease and pest problems. If you live in a humid area, you'll have better luck with roses grown for mildew resistance.

Roses

Common Rose Diseases

❑ Black Spot ❑ Botrytis ❑ Canker ❑ Crown Gall ❑ Downy Mildew ❑ Mosaic
❑ Powdery Mildew ❑ Rust ❑ Spot Anthracnose

Roses

Common Rose Pests

❑ Aphids ❑ Borers ❑ Japanese Beetles ❑ Leaf-cutting Bees ❑ Leaf Rollers ❑ Midges
❑ Nematodes ❑ Rose Scales ❑ Rose Slugs ❑ Spider Mites ❑ Thrips

Winterizing Your Roses

If you live in an area where temperatures drop below freezing, you'll have to provide some protection for your roses. Different roses require different amounts of "winterizing." For example, China, tea, and most pale-colored hybrid tea, grandiflora, and floribunda roses are especially susceptible to winter's frigid air. Most climbing and miniature roses can survive unprotected in temperatures to 0° F. Old garden and shrub roses are quite hardy and only need protection in locations where the temperatures drop to -10° F.

The best time to winterize your roses is in the fall right after the ground freezes. Some common methods include mulching with additional soil, covering roses with evergreen boughs (a good way to recycle your Christmas tree), and covering the plants with oak leaves. Oak leaves work especially well with the very tender tree roses. To protect tree roses, drive four stakes into the ground around the plant and securely wrap burlap around the stakes. Fill the area inside the burlap with oak leaves or shredded newspaper. Be sure to cover the entire plant.

If you have climbing roses and live in an area where temperatures drop below zero, you'll have to remove the plants from their supports and fasten them to the ground. Use soil, leaves, or burlap wrap to protect the delicate canes.

If you live in the very coldest section of the country, you may have to protect your roses with plastic or foam cones. You can purchase these at most cold climate zone garden stores. Prune the plants to fit under the cone after the ground freezes, then cover and place a rock on top of the cone to keep it from blowing over. Take the cone off during winter's warmer days to avoid stimulating early plant growth. Remove the cone completely and store for the next year after all chances of freezing temperatures are over.

Rose Care Tips

- It is important to dead-head once a week. Leave at least two sets of five-leaflet leaves on the new shoot when you cut a rose on most varieties. This encourages more flowering and prevents the formation of rose hips.
- In the All-America Rose Selections display garden at the Hub in the Magic Kingdom Park, to the right of Cinderella Castle, a regular six-week fertilization schedule keeps the roses in top condition and in full bloom.
- The major pest problems at Walt Disney World Resort are red spider mites during dry conditions and black spot in the rainy season. Biocontrols, such as predatory mites, are successful in controlling the red spider mites. Fungicides applied at the recommended rates for good results are Daconyl, Mancozeb, Benomyl, and copper fungicides.
- After heavily pruning back rose bushes, be sure to mulch them well. During the winter months in northern climates, also mulch around the base of rose bushes.
- Because of growing problems specific to the deep south (e.g., year-round season, humidity, disease, and insect problems) Rosa fortuniana is the preferred rootstock at Walt Disney World Resort.
- Use the right tools and keep them sharpened, oiled, and clean. To reduce the spread of disease, wipe pruners off with ethyl alcohol after each use.
- Check weekly for pest and disease troubles.

The Versatile Garden Choice

Roses are the most popular of all the plants for a variety of reasons. They can create a dramatic background cascading luxuriantly over a fence, become a dramatic focal point or brilliant spot of color when planted alone or in pots, and make stunning hedges, borders, and ground covers when planted together in rows. If you plant annuals around your roses you have the exciting option of changing the color scheme with the seasons. Planting perennials and bulbs among the roses gives you continuously changing color.

Many roses fill the air with their heady fragrance, inviting you to take deep breaths of their intoxicating perfume. If you plant roses near the patio, porch, or picnic seating areas, you can really enjoy the scent. Cut a few stems to bring indoors for vases and make potpourri from the petals as they dry.

If you're short on space, try growing roses in containers. Miniature and low-growing floribunda roses are nicely suited to life in a container. You can also move the containers around for a quick decorating change. Be sure to keep them well watered and fertilized.

Many roses grow very dense and provide the perfect disguise for unsightly areas of the yard. For example, a pool pump, air conditioning unit, trash cans, or garden shed can be camouflaged easily with climbing or floribunda roses planted next to them. Roses are long-lasting, fragrant, produce gorgeous blooms in an infinite number of shapes and shades, are easy to grow and care for, and are extremely versatile.

TRIVIA

- It is believed that roses have existed for about 15 million years! The Chinese started cultivating them 5,000 years ago.
- Walt Disney World Resort is one of the 116 national gardens where the current year's All-America Rose Selection (AARS) winners can be viewed before going on sale to the public in late December.
- Display roses in the All-America Rose Selections (AARS) Official Test Garden in the Magic Kingdom are changed every two years.
- Gardeners in EPCOT spend eight hours per week (that's 400 hours a year!) removing spent blooms from the rose gardens.
- The colorful rose hips (fruit) of shrub roses like Bonica add interest to winter landscapes, attract song birds, and are a flavorful source of vitamin C.
- Rosa banksiae, named for Lady Banks, arrived in Britain from China in 1807. This lovely climber, found in a collection of Old World roses at United Kingdom in EPCOT, is truly unusual since it has been bred to have an almost thornless stem.
- Miniature roses blossom on Main Street, U.S.A. in Disneyland Park and in window boxes, hanging baskets, and even indoors in EPCOT.
- A mix of red, yellow, and white miniature roses add color to boxwood parterres at United Kingdom in EPCOT.
- Morocco is a major exporter to France of 'Sonya' roses for perfumes. You'll find these roses growing in containers between Morocco and France in EPCOT.
- Guests at Pleasure Island stroll through a formal waterside rose garden just behind the Portobello Yacht Club restaurant.

Geraniums ta
on a regal
appearance i
an ornate
container.

Container gardens are really gardens in miniature, adding living color, creating a mood, or accenting an entryway, balcony, porch, pool area, or deck. They also provide space-cramped apartment-dwellers a chance to show-off a green thumb and add softness and life to sometimes stark urban settings. Many people easily grow flowers, trees, shrubs, vegetables, and herbs in containers. Gardeners with physical limitations can also maintain fantastic container gardens with a little ingenuity.

Potted annuals add a festival of color in New Orleans Square *in* Disneyland Park.

You can create "walls of color" by placing containers or trellises of tall plants next to a fence or wall or by letting vining plants "climb." You can also rearrange container gardens to "redecorate" every so often. They are low-cost, easy to maintain, and grow quickly. They're portable when you move or when it gets cold, and can deliver an immediate and stunning display of color and texture. Container plantings enhance elements of the architecture, create color "splashes," accentuate the theme of a particular area, and complement existing landscaping. The versatility of container gardening is amazing!

Selecting the Container

Container selection is very important. Be sure the container's size and proportion is appropriate for the type and amount of plants you're adding as well as the setting the container will be placed in. Decide if you want it to match or contrast with the color and style of your home. If you have a modern-style dwelling, you probably don't want to select an old-fashioned half-barrel planter. If you're planting a very Oriental-looking plant, why not select a lovely Oriental-patterned container? Some new Fiberglas™ and plastic containers look convincingly like Italian terra-cotta pots and are striking next to a pool or on a patio. Consider a planter with wheels if you are planning a large or heavy container. Remember, wet soil is extremely heavy, so ease of moving a container is a must.

Try wooden barrels for a rustic, country feel.

The material the container is made of also has significance in your selection. Clay pots have a tendency to dry out more quickly than certain other types of containers. You'll have to water more frequently if you plant in a clay container, especially if you live in a hot, windy, or dry area, because the clay is very porous.

Large containers can create show-stopping focal points.

Flowers cascade from this New Orleans Square balcony in Disneyland Park.

Overwatering, which leads to root rot, can also be a problem if you're using any container with inadequate or no drainage holes, especially those made of plastic or cement. If necessary, poke a larger hole or additional holes in your container before planting, so your plants won't be left standing in water.

Pink geraniums accented with floral "skirts" grace Germany in EPCOT.

Creative Containers

Bags of soil
(Plant right in the bag)
Barrels
Boxes
Bowls
Buckets
Cement containers
Ceramic pots
Clay pots
Coconut shells
Garbage cans
Glass containers
Hanging baskets
Hollowed-out logs
Old rowboats
Peck and bushel fruit baskets
Plastic pails
Tubs
Urns
Wheelbarrows
Wire baskets

Selecting the Plants

You're really showcasing plants when you put them in containers. They take on a special beauty and character, almost as if the container is a stage and the plants are the actors and actresses. Their structures, colors, textures, and individual characteristics are accentuated once they are spotlighted in a special setting.

Palm trees look right at home in these terra-cotta pots.

When planning your container, select plants with similar light, watering, and environmental needs. For example, use tough-foliaged plants for windy or hot areas. Keep scale and height in mind — don't place tall-growing plants in front of low-growing plants or quickly spreading plants near slowly spreading ones. You may also want to incorporate perennials into your container and replant annuals around the edges as the seasons change.

Consider flower color, leaf shape and size, texture, final size of the plant, and container location. Ask yourself what you want to accomplish. Are you adding color? Covering a bare spot? Creating a "look"? Raising fruit or vegetables? Growing herbs? Is the container going to be permanent, lasting through the seasons, or a seasonal display that can be replaced with evergreens during the winter months? What is your goal?

Try unusual plant combinations for impressive results.

A mix of herbs and plants is both practical and pretty.

Closely nestled containers offer an eclectic welcome at Italy in EPCOT.

Container Gardens

Tips for Container Garden Selections

- Save "busy" flowers for containers. Plants that are high maintenance (for example, in need of frequent "deadheading") can be used in container gardens where they are easily accessed.
- Planted containers can be used as a privacy screen or to control traffic flow across patio or pool areas.
- For city dwellers lacking in space, try hanging window boxes, wall brackets, and sturdy wall shelving to add life to those empty garden walls.
- You can plant a container garden any time of year. For instance, window boxes can be planted with bulbs in the fall for an early spring display.

Planting Container Gardens

The Soil

Soil mixture requirements vary based on the types of plants you use and the weight of the mix combined with the weight of the container. Drainage and aeration are important since all of the moisture and air have to enter the soil mix at the upper surface. If the soil is too fine, an impervious upper layer will result and moisture will not reach the root system. Use soil amendments for their root support, aeration, drainage, and moisture retention abilities. Just be certain to adjust your maintenance schedule and water more frequently when choosing a light-weight mix that dries out quickly.

Sun-loving lantana is colorful and hardy.

If you live in a condo, apartment, or don't have enough space to make your own potting mix, you can buy prepared potting mix for seedlings and small pots. You'll need only a hand trowel to do your planting. If you intend to do a lot of containers or trees and shrubs, it's probably best and the most economical to make your own potting mix. This is an easy, but messy task, so find a suitable location where a little dirt won't upset anyone. The only tool you need is a shovel. Clean-up will go quickly if you mix your soil on top of an old sheet or large plastic covering.

Lightweight Mix for Seedlings and Pots

- ❑ 1 cubic foot each of peat moss, vermiculite, and perlite
- ❑ ½ pound 5-10-5 fertilizer
- ❑ ½ pound ground limestone

Shrub and Tree Mix

- ❑ 2½ cubic feet ground bark or nitrogen-stabilized sawdust
- ❑ 1 cubic foot coarse sand
- ❑ ½ pound 5-10-10 fertilizer
- ❑ ¾ pound ground limestone
- ❑ 2 oz. iron sulfate

The fertilizer breaks down over time, so only make up as much soil mix as you need at a time. You can adjust the mix ratio for more or less, as necessary.

A container-grown bougainvillea can be easily trained into a single trunk.

Adding the Plants

Possibly the most important step before planting is to ensure your container will provide adequate drainage. Most manufactured clay and plastic pots have at least one sufficient drainage hole, but there is one more procedure you should do before you add your soil mix and plants. Place an inch or more of a coarse aggregate, like pea gravel, rocks, or clay pot shards, at the bottom of your container.

Lushly growing periwinkles embellish the Neptune fountain area in EPCOT.

The number and type of plants you add will depend upon how large the container is, where it will be located, and what type of look you're aiming for. Consider each container as a visual composition of plants. In a grouping of plants, look at the whole group as a single picture to convey a theme. Typically, container garden plants are packed in more tightly than if you were planting them directly in the ground. Use your own judgement, but remember to keep tall plants behind plants of medium height, and use low-growing, hanging, or cascading plants as an edging apron in front.

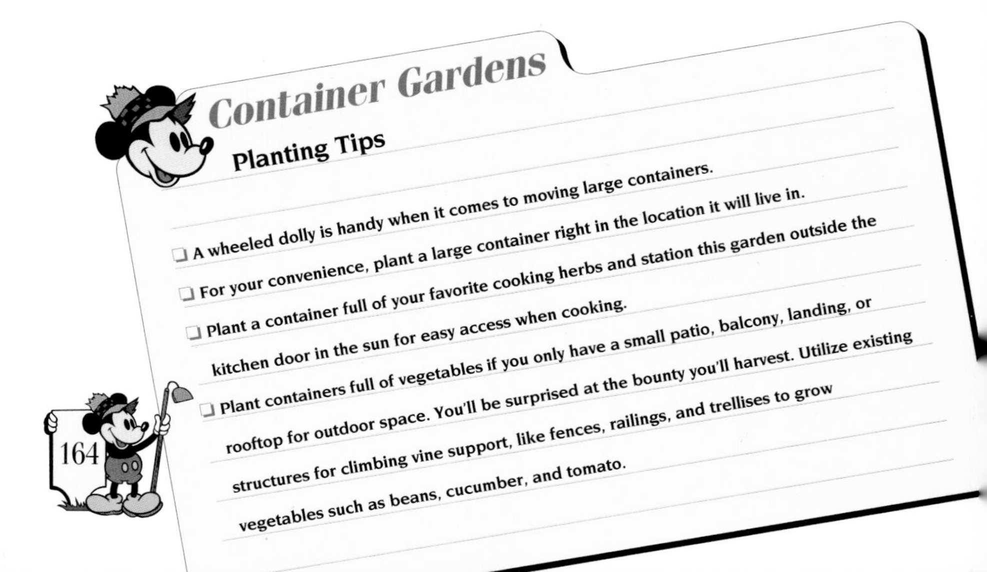

Container Gardens

Planting Tips

- A wheeled dolly is handy when it comes to moving large containers.
- For your convenience, plant a large container right in the location it will live in.
- Plant a container full of your favorite cooking herbs and station this garden outside the kitchen door in the sun for easy access when cooking.
- Plant containers full of vegetables if you only have a small patio, balcony, landing, or rooftop for outdoor space. You'll be surprised at the bounty you'll harvest. Utilize existing structures for climbing vine support, like fences, railings, and trellises to grow vegetables such as beans, cucumber, and tomato.

If you're planting containers for indoors, remember that many plants need a sunny window or at least a very bright location to look their best. Check light preferences before planting and group plants with similar cultural requirements together.

A variety of container plants add tropical ambiance to Disney's Grand Floridian Beach Resort.

A brass container adds formal appeal to this flowering azalea.

Caring for Container Gardens

Adequate water and fertilizer, plus just enough pinching and pruning will keep your container gardens in peak form. As a general rule, don't allow container gardens to dry out. Water thoroughly, but don't create a soggy environment for your plants either. Check the container each day to see if it's dry and water accordingly. You may need to water twice a day in hot and/or dry climates. Container gardens resting on paved surfaces tend to dry out especially quickly because heat and light reflects from buildings and pavement. If you are planning extensive container gardening endeavors, you may want to install plastic tubing irrigation and set the water schedule on an automatic timeclock for convenience.

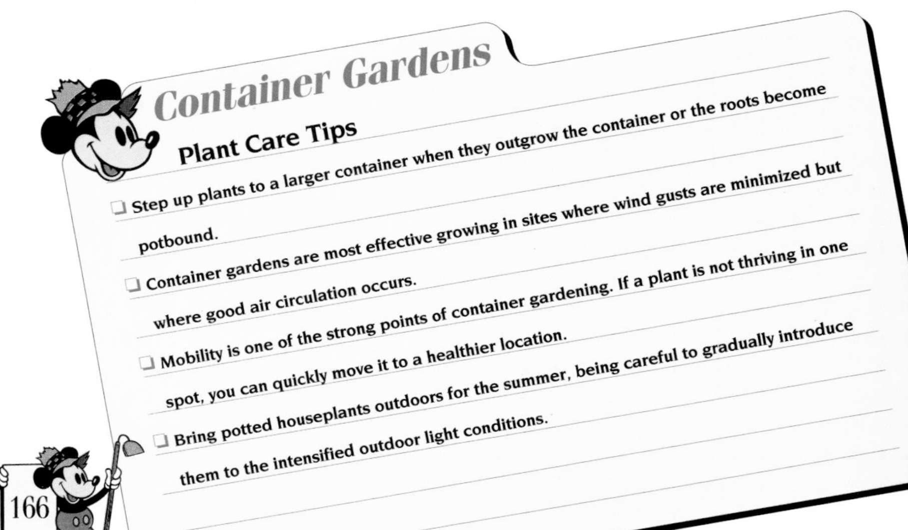

Container Gardens

Plant Care Tips

- Step up plants to a larger container when they outgrow the container or the roots become potbound.
- Container gardens are most effective growing in sites where wind gusts are minimized but where good air circulation occurs.
- Mobility is one of the strong points of container gardening. If a plant is not thriving in one spot, you can quickly move it to a healthier location.
- Bring potted houseplants outdoors for the summer, being careful to gradually introduce them to the intensified outdoor light conditions.

Cacti thrive in unusual containers in Tomorrowland in Disneyland Park.

Watering container gardens can cause the fertilizers to be flushed out of the soil very rapidly. Container-grown plants also have limited root run and are closely spaced, so feed the plants every two to three weeks with either water-soluble or time-release fertilizer. Pinching faded blooms not only maintains a neat appearance, it encourages growth, too. It's also important to stake plants when the stems become tall and top-heavy.

If you have any physical limitations that cause trouble when bending, kneeling, or lifting, plant waist-high container gardens. Locate them conveniently near a door, outside a window, or on a patio or balcony to save time and exertion. Proximity to water is important, too. Garden hoses and full watering cans can be very heavy. A drip irrigation system would be a possible option. Select plants requiring minimal upkeep and those that grow at a moderate pace to save on maintenance time.

How to Create an Instant Spring Garden

What You'll Need

- ❑ Three 4" blooming plants (choose three different varieties)
- ❑ One 12" container with adequate drain holes
- ❑ 5-10-10 granular fertilizer
- ❑ Pea gravel
- ❑ 2-quart bag of potting soil
- ❑ Coarse-grained sand

Place a small amount of gravel at the bottom of the container to aid with drainage and to prevent soil from washing away.

Mix a few handfuls of sand with the soil to assure fast drainage and a porous soil mixture. Mix in two tablespoons of fertilizer to boost blooming.

Create a tiny bit of paradise with a glorious combination of annuals.

3 Add soil to within 1" of the rim of the container. Plant the plants and firm the soil around each rootball. Water immediately.

4 Test soil moisture by poking your finger into the soil. If it's dry beneath the surface, it's time to water. Heavy watering leaches out plant nutrients, so light and frequent feedings are preferable.

Window Boxes

Trailing plants add certain charm to window boxes.

Window boxes can give a home real character. A plain home can take on the appearance of a Swiss chalet or country cottage with little effort and a minimum of upkeep. In Disneyland Park, for example, a Bavarian theme is accented with window boxes filled with red, pink, and white geraniums.

As long as you maintain a good watering, pinching, and fertilizing schedule you'll be blessed with bountiful blooms for many months. As the seasons change, window boxes can be easily replanted giving you a fresh look every so often.

Some window boxes are set on the window sill or ledge and others are bolted securely. Whatever kind of window

These "window boxes" are actually attached to the balcony railing.

Petunias flourish in street-level window boxes.

box you have, the most important considerations are drainage and light. It is imperative the box has multiple holes to allow for water runoff. Putting a small square of screening material over the holes prevents the soil from escaping with the water.

When selecting plants, determine how much and what kind of light the window box will receive. Southern and western exposures require hardier plants that can tolerate more sun and drier conditions. Northern exposure is typically quite shady, cool, and moist and an eastern exposure's morning sun usually provides just the right amount of light without excessive drying.

For really quick changes, insert potted plants directly into the window box — pot and all! Remember to water these plants at least once a day because they dry out more quickly when they remain in pots.

The Fall "Mum Show"

During October and November at the Magic Kingdom Park and EPCOT, colorful "waterfalls" of cascading chrysanthemums ("mums") adorn walls and staircases, draped like heavy, living blankets. Vast expanses of bedding mums, floating containers of mums, round baskets of mums, and unusual tree-like mums (called "standards") are also in their full glory, but it is the cascading mums that really capture the imagination. This fleeting spectacle is really something to behold.

Creating the cascading autumnal display is a year-round process for Disney horticulturists. The plants must be selected, rooted, forced, misted, staked, tricked, transplanted, pinched, tied, fertilized, watered, trimmed, cut back, monitored, and pampered in a strict regimen.

The elaborate procedure begins around March 1 when 2" to 3" cuttings are taken from plants that were started the previous August. The cuttings are dipped in rooting hormone to encourage strong root formation, then gently placed into a mixture of peat and perlite that has been drenched with a 20-20-20 general purpose fertilizer. The cuttings are misted with water for four seconds every four minutes for two weeks. At night, the cuttings are exposed to light from 10 p.m. to 2 a.m. to inhibit flower bud development.

Lush carpets of mums adorn stair railings at Japan in EPCOT.

Once the cuttings are rooted, they are replanted into 4" pots. The mums grow to about 8" to 10" tall by April and are then ready to be staked and loosely tied. Gardeners carefully watch for insects and soil-borne fungi and maintain a preventive control program.

The four hours of nightly light stops at the end of March, but the pampering is a continuous process.

By the beginning of June, the mums are 2' to 3' tall and ready to be transplanted into either one- or three-gallon containers. The mums are planted close to one edge of the pot in a leaning position toward the rim. The plants are allowed to wilt so the stems can be delicately bent downward and attached to a special wire frame with S-hooks. This frame acts as a support to the growing and spreading plant, helping to create the "cascade" look of the fully grown mums. The plants are fertilized regularly and monitored for burned leaf tips.

Cuttings are snipped from the plants and taken away to start next year's plants in early August. As this year's plants continue to grow, the lateral growth is pinched or sheared until the end of August to mid-September to encourage a dense cascade. This new growth is spread out horizontally and secured to the frame with S-hooks.

The final shearing and pinching occurs in mid-September and then a growth retardant is applied to prevent flower buds from forming too quickly. Later that month, a 10-30-20 fertilizer is applied to encourage bud development. In early October, nitrogen applications are stopped to prolong blossom life, but all other fertilizing continues.

In the middle of the night in late October, when all the cascades are just beginning to bloom, they are moved into their positions in Magic Kingdom and EPCOT. The next morning, Park guests are treated to their first glimpse of this incredible seasonal display.

Colorful flower "dots" float on an EPCOT pond.

Floating Planters

Throughout Walt Disney Theme Parks and Resorts you'll notice lush containers of plants and flowers seemingly floating on the water. You can easily create this special illusion in your own landscape if you have a pool, pond, or small lake. The floating planters at Walt Disney World Resort have water absorbent capillary matting and a water wick to minimize the necessity of hand-watering. At Disneyland Park, the floating containers are created using a different method using no water wick and must be watered once a week.

At Disneyland Park, tall-growing coreopsis, foxglove, delphinium, or penstemon are used for the center of the planter, while pansy, impatiens, or paludosum daisy are often selected for planting around the center plants. At Walt Disney World Resort, tropical-looking philodendron 'Xanadu,' New Guinea impatiens, and Boston fern grow in floating containers.

Container Gardens

Floating Planter Tips

- Vary the height, type, and color of plants for an interesting contrast.
- Place the tallest plants in the middle since the breeze will twirl the planter around in the water. This pyramidal layering of plants will also set them off to their best advantage from all sides.
- Ducks and other birds often find floating gardens inviting nesting or dining sites. If you discover birds in your container, remove the container for a while and then put it back after a few days. Hopefully, your feathered friends will have discovered a new home by then. If necessary, buy a "duck guard" to keep the birds from nibbling on your plants.
- Plant cascading plant varieties, like ivy, around the edge of the container to hide the container and also to create a soft edge.

Floating planters gently drifting around anchor-free in a reflecting or swimming pool look beautiful for a special occasion. You can create a simple floating planter by inserting a clay, plastic, or ceramic pot through a foam ring, making sure the ring is large enough to hold the planted and watered pot above the water level. Use a container without drainage holes because the soil will dirty the water and may disrupt a pool's delicate chemical balance. Chlorinated pool water could also "wick up" into the plants, burning the roots or possibly killing the plants.

Floating planters enhance the fairy-tale setting of Disneyland Park.

Bright orange chrysanthemums drift on tranquil water at China in EPCOT.

People aren't the only living creatures to admire floating gardens.

How to Make a Water Wick Floating Planter

What You'll Need

- ❑ One unpainted Styrofoam™ disk (2" x 4" ring mounted on a 4" x 36" round base)
- ❑ Black acrylic interior/exterior spray paint
- ❑ Florist's knife
- ❑ Sharp scissors
- ❑ 1"-thick capillary mat, 36" x 40" piece
- ❑ 1" washers for anchors
- ❑ 4" eye bolt with bolt nut and nylon cord
- ❑ Anchor (fill a plastic gallon container with sand or water)
- ❑ Up to fifty 4" bedding plants or one 1-gallon tropical plant and twenty 4" plants
- ❑ 1½ cubic yards light soilless potting mix

Spray the floater black.

Cut a 1" diameter hole in the bottom of the disk. Cut a 36" round piece of capillary matting and line the bottom of the disk. Be sure to cut a 1" diameter hole through the capillary mat, too.

3 Cut a 1" wide strip of capillary matting and insert it through the hole in the bottom of the disk to act as a water wick. Allow the strip to hang 8-10" below the disk and insert the other end through the liner, knotting the strip at the top to secure the wick to the mat.

4 Fasten a 4" eye bolt with the bolt nut and 1" washers for anchoring the disk once it is in place to keep the planter from straying too far.

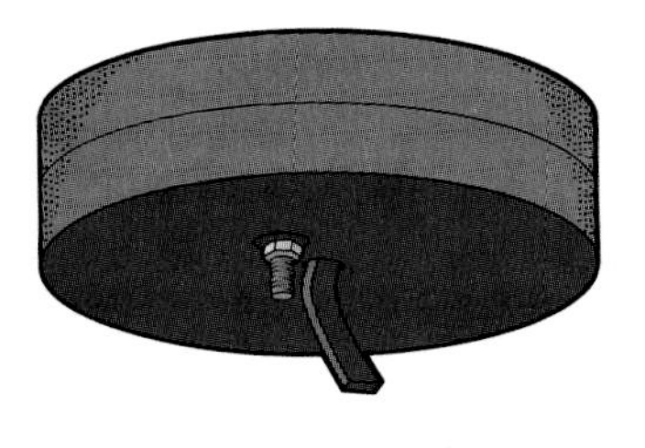

5 Add the potting mix and plant with appropriate plants. Use up to fifty 4" bedding plants for a floral floater or for a tropical floater use one 1-gallon focal plant in the center and surround it with twenty 4" plants around the edge.

6 Anchor your floating planter, making sure the nylon cord is long enough so that the anchor rests on the bottom of the water location.

Vegetables to Grow in Containers

Artichoke
Asparagus
Beans
Beets
Broccoli
Brussels Sprouts
Cabbage

Carrots
Cauliflower
Celery
Corn
Cucumber

Eggplant
Garlic
Kale
Leeks
Lettuce
Okra
Onion
Peas
Peppers
Potato
Radish
Rhubarb
Shallot
Spinach
Squash
Sweet Potato

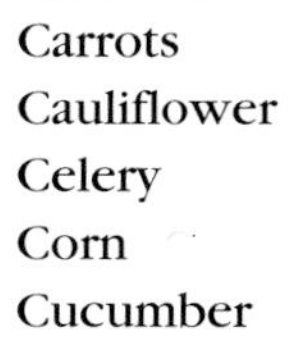

Swiss Chard
Tomato
Turnip
Zucchini

Herbs to Grow in Containers

- Basil
- Bay
- Borage
- Burnet
- Catnip
- Chives
- Cilantro
- Comfrey
- Coriander
- Dill
- Marjoram
- Mint
- Oregano
- Parsley
- Rosemary
- Sage
- Summer Savory
- Tarragon
- Thyme
- Watercress
- Winter Savory

T R I V I A

- In Disneyland Park, floating gardens featuring a spinning hippo and a crocodile who spurts water, entertain guests near the Fantasia Garden.

- Disney gardeners use leftover Styrofoam™ "peanuts" used for packing in the troughs and barrel planters of annuals in EPCOT. A soil mix of "peanuts" is lighter in weight, more economical, and improves drainage better than conventional soil mixes.

- The chefs in Disney-MGM Studios Theme Park often add some spice to their culinary creations by picking herbs like rosemary and thyme on the corners of Hollywood and Vine.

- At Germany and Italy in EPCOT there are interesting contrasts in container gardening styles. At Germany, a single plant (such as a a bright red geranium) is planted in profusion to make a bold statement. At Italy, it's anything goes! You'll see a mixture of variegated vinca minor, Sophie ivy geraniums, white verbena, and light blue brachycome, all in one pot.

- Culinary and medicinal herbs flourish in containers in the Frontierland Pioneer House in Disneyland Park.

- The smallest container gardens in Walt Disney World Resort are found at Japan in EPCOT. There is a dwarf azalea living in a 6" pot in the bonsai collection.

- If you were to stretch your imagination, you could say the largest container garden in Walt Disney World Resort is the large oval in front of the Disney-MGM Studios Theme Park ticket booths. It holds a volume of 1,000 cubic feet of soil and requires 875 4" bedding plants to look its best.

- The wide, winding stairs of the Disney Gallery in New Orleans Square in Disneyland Park are seasonally decked with potted cyclamen, chrysanthemums, daffodils, or tulips.

- Need some patio garden ideas? There are over 140 container gardens at Italy in EPCOT featuring a dazzling array of colorful bedding plants.

- Pyramid-shaped privet thrive in containers in the courtyard of Sleeping Beauty Castle in Disneyland Park.

Masses of impatiens blossoms creat[e] a quaint, eye-level foca[l] point.

You just can't miss them! Those gorgeous hanging baskets, overflowing with colorful flowers and luxuriant greenery, always demand attention, even amidst the pageantry, music, and other visual excitement all around you.

Hundreds of hanging baskets create eye-level accents, enhance the beauty of the surroundings, and complement the many colorful flower beds throughout the Disney Parks and Resorts. Hanging baskets enrich the themes and accentuate the architecture of dozens of locations, punctuating sleek, futuristic buildings with spots of living color, adding subtle detail to nostalgic recreations of the past, and helping to create inviting spaces for pleasant relaxation.

A dazzling combination of flowers is combined for a rainbow of color.

At Disneyland Park, pastel-colored petunia or primrose baskets decorate the "Hub" area in the Central Plaza year 'round. The baskets complement flower beds at ground level, drawing your eye upward to the soft-hued towers of the fairy-tale Sleeping Beauty Castle high in the sky. Luxuriant hanging baskets of exotic plants, like tropical orchids and anthurium, help put the adventure in Adventureland on the patio of the Enchanted Tiki Room.

Hanging baskets seem right at home on Main Street, U.S.A. in the Magic Kingdom Park at Walt Disney World Resort. Springtime on Main Street, U.S.A. brings Victorian "bouquets" brimming with flowers hung from the vintage street's old-fashioned gas lights. Summer heralds patriotic red, white, and

Vibrant colors contrast dramatically with the leafy, green background.

blue floral combinations, intensifying the feeling of hometown America at the turn of the century. In a given year, different collections of matched baskets — each carefully planned to look their best for the appropriate season — are placed on display along Main Street, U.S.A.

In Adventureland, exotic blends of foliage, with jungle-like texture, lush growth, and bright splashes of color underscore the tropical motif. Baskets in this jungle paradise may contain such unusual combinations as 'White Wing' caladium, 'Fiery Tails' acalypha, and sprawling spider plants — all encouraged to grow dense and untamed, just like they would in the wild.

In front of Cinderella Castle, the "Hub" of the Magic Kingdom, hanging baskets are a focal point throughout the year. Yellow and blue pansies blossom in winter, leafy "balls" of wax begonias in spring are followed by striped "beach balls" of alternanthera that last through the summer, and then traditional holiday displays of mums and poinsettias bring in the holiday season.

Some plants, like fern and cyclamen, prefer a shady spot.

At The American Adventure at EPCOT, bell-shaped, three-foot-long English ivy baskets convey the holiday spirit around the Christmas season. At Disney-MGM Studios Theme Park you'll be surprised by a humorous application for hanging baskets. Carefully selected blue flowers in the buckets of the "Dancing Brooms" simulate splashing water as the "brooms" dash away.

Hanging baskets are simple to create and many of the Disney techniques can be applied successfully by home gardeners. These "living spots of color" can soften the sharp edges of a balcony, accent a flower bed, complement your home's color scheme, or add charm to a front porch. Careful planning, timely planting, and diligent care pay off in great rewards for the hanging basket gardener.

Lamppost Baskets Around the Year

Choose a single lamppost at any location in the Magic Kingdom Park and you will see a transformation from season to season. Disney gardeners stealthily change the baskets during the wee hours of the morning before the Park opens to announce a new season or the beginning of the holidays. The total number of baskets produced for just the Magic Kingdom Park to accomplish this change is over 2,400 baskets per year! Pansies and alyssum may herald the coming of spring. Brilliantly colored impatiens might set the scene for summer. Chrysanthemums may foretell autumn's approach, while poinsettias usually adorn the lampposts during the winter holidays. A single lamppost may undergo as many as six seasonal and holiday changes throughout the year. All of this activity is carefully coordinated months in advance by Disney horticulturists who plan according to time of year, architecture, and theming needs of each specific location.

Kalaidescopic blooms add an enchanting touch.

Pink mandevilla baskets accent the Italy pavilion in EPCOT.

Selecting Plants for Hanging Baskets

To ensure success, Disney gardeners recommend you select plants with certain characteristics when creating hanging baskets. For example, habit of growth is an important factor. Plants with a naturally cascading habit are often chosen for hanging baskets because they tumble over the container creating a wonderful waterfall of color.

You'll see fast rewards if you select plants that grow and fill in quickly. This is especially important for home gardeners living in areas with short growing seasons. Beautiful, long-lasting blossom color is another key element in plant selection. Attractive flowering characteristics and resistance to pest problems are also desirable and sought-after traits you should consider.

Plants you select must also be appropriate for the specific season and their final hanging destination. Shade-loving plants shouldn't end up in a sunny spot and sun-tolerant plants won't thrive if relegated to a shady locale. Plants must also work together proportionally. This means that one plant should not grow too quickly dominating the slower-growing plants and blocking their source of light.

Abundantly flowering impatiens are always a popular hanging basket choice.

Disney gardeners make their selections from specific plant cultivars for the appropriate season and to provide the best color, texture, and longevity as possible. Cultivars are horticulturally or agriculturally derived varieties of plants raised for particular traits. By selecting a specific cultivar, you can expect your flowers to do what you want when you want them to do it. Plant labels often list cultivar names or you can order specific cultivars from plant catalogs for your own particular region.

Brilliant bougainvillea flowers are beautifully showcased against its unique foliage.

Mickey's Favorite Plant Combinations for Sphagnum Hanging Baskets

For a touch of green...

Boston 'Compacta' Fern
(Nephrolepis exaltata 'Compacta')
Asparagus Fern
(Asparagus sprengerii)
'White Wing' Caladium
(C. x hortulanum 'White Wing')

For seasonal accents...

Poinsettia
(Euphorbia pulcherrima)
Spider Plant
(Chlorophytum comosum)
Wax Begonia
(Begonia x semperflorens cultorum Hybrids)

Colorful perennial favorites...

Bougainvillea
(Bougainvillea spectabilis cvs.)
Lantana
(Lantana camara)
Verbena
(Verbena spp.)
Mandevilla
(Mandevilla x amabilis 'Alice du Pont')
Chenille Plant
(Acalypha hispida)

For a tropical touch...

Boston Fern
(Nephrolepis exaltata)
Caladium
(Caladium x hortulanum)
Chenille Plant
(Acalypha hispida)

For a round ball...

Browallia
(Browallia speciosa)
Wax Begonia
(Begonia x semperflorens cultorum Hybrids.)

For a floral bouquet...

Dianthus
(Dianthus chinensis)
Browallia
(Browallia speciosa)
Alyssum
(Lobularia maritima)
Lobelia
(Lobelia species)
Impatiens
(Impatiens wallerana)

For a floral cascade...

Petunia 'Red Cascade'
(P. x hybrida 'Cascade Series')
Petunia 'White Cascade'
(P. x hybrida 'Cascade Series')
Petunia 'Blue Cascade'
(P. x hybrida 'Cascade Series')

Creating a Hanging Basket

Huge globes of yellow chrysanthemums mark autumn's return.

At Walt Disney World Resort and Disneyland Park, hanging baskets are produced behind the scenes at the Nursery. Baskets are scheduled and grown for a certain location and a specific season or holiday. Additional baskets are maintained as backups in case of plant loss and some are grown as "test baskets" of new cultivar, color, or plant combinations.

All baskets are produced with sphagnum primarily for aesthetic reasons, but it is also used because it helps retard fungus, holds the soil in efficiently, and hides the wire frame of the basket well. The sphagnum baskets are planted in two different ways: (1) plants are grown from the top only and allowed to cascade over the sides; and (2) plants are grown from the sides as well as the top of the basket to create a "ball" effect. Baskets planted using this second method can be produced in less time and the end result is often a more voluminous basket. Plastic baskets are utilized in areas requiring a no-drip pot, such as above walkways or dining locations.

The wire hangers on both sphagnum and plastic pots must be replaced occasionally due to the corrosive action of regular watering, fertilizing, and constant exposure to the elements. The baskets also need a sturdy hanging support because they can weigh 20 to 60 pounds when fully watered.

Cascading ivy geraniums tumble over the edge of this hanging basket.

How to Make a Sphagnum Hanging Basket

What You'll Need

- ❑ A 10-14" wire basket
- ❑ Unmilled sphagnum moss
- ❑ Gloves
- ❑ Bucket

1 Moisten several handfuls of sphagnum moss by immersing it in a bucket of water (be sure to wear gloves when handling sphagnum moss).

2 Begin stuffing the moss into the basket, starting with the bottom and working towards the top. Be careful to stuff the moss securely between each "rung" of the wire basket.

3 Attach a wire hanger to the rim of the basket.

4 Now your basket is ready to plant!

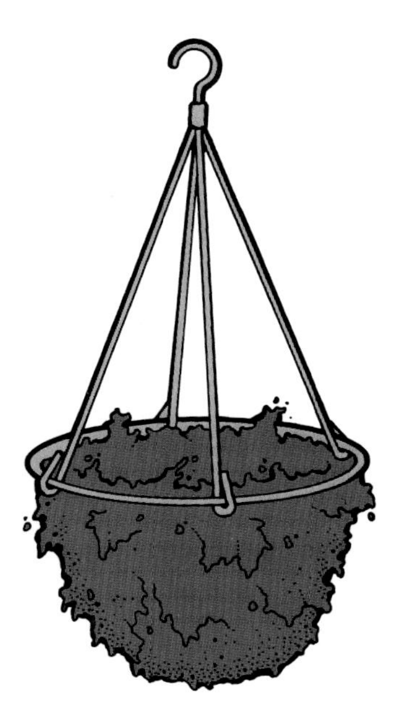

How to Plant a Begonia Ball Hanging Basket

What You'll Need

- ❑ A 10-14" wire basket prestuffed with sphagnum moss
- ❑ A 2-quart bag of potting soil
- ❑ 12 small wax begonia plants or rooted cuttings
- ❑ 1 tablespoon granular, slow-release fertilizer (like 14-14-14)

Flowery wax begonia balls are appealing and simple to create.

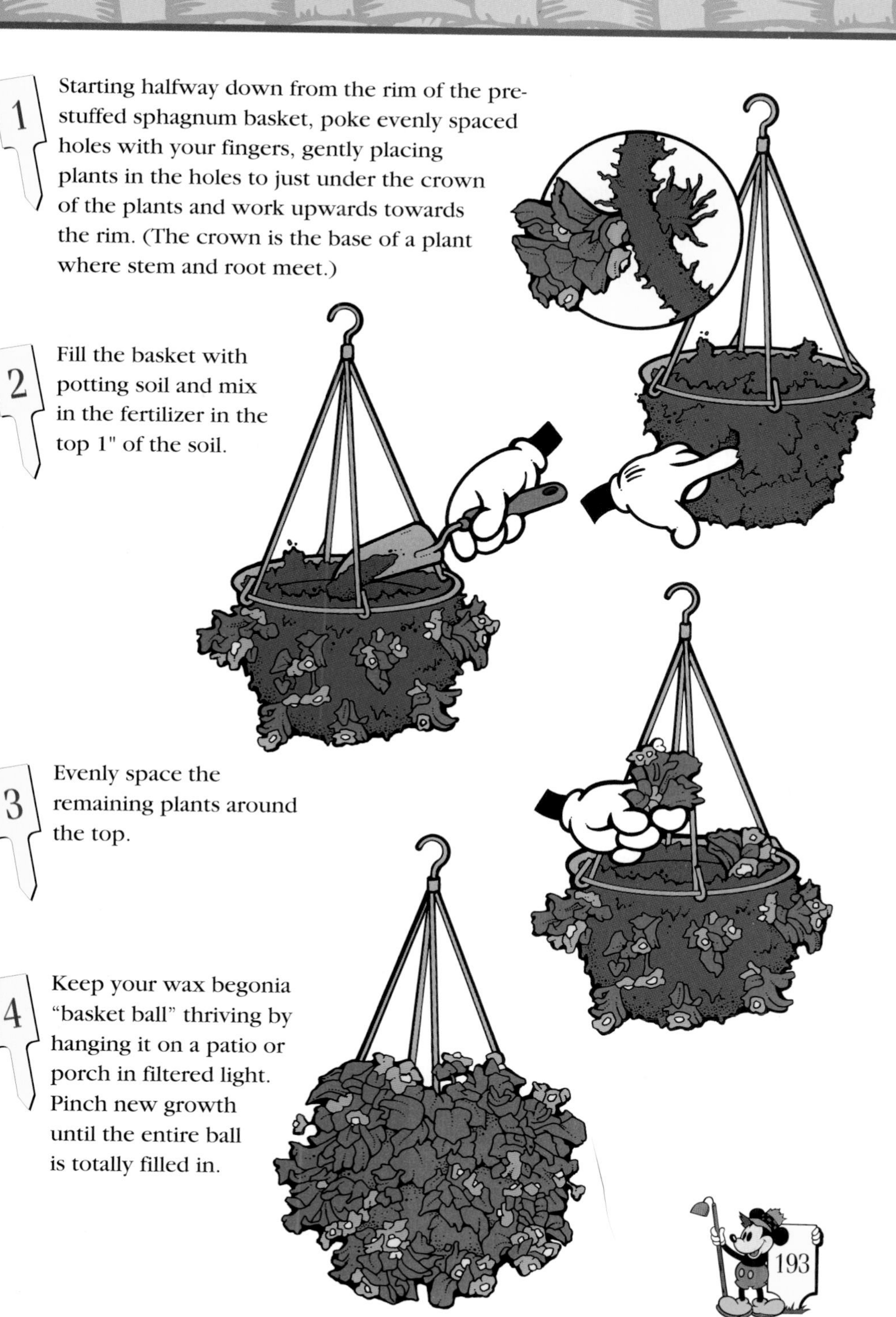

1 Starting halfway down from the rim of the prestuffed sphagnum basket, poke evenly spaced holes with your fingers, gently placing plants in the holes to just under the crown of the plants and work upwards towards the rim. (The crown is the base of a plant where stem and root meet.)

2 Fill the basket with potting soil and mix in the fertilizer in the top 1" of the soil.

3 Evenly space the remaining plants around the top.

4 Keep your wax begonia "basket ball" thriving by hanging it on a patio or porch in filtered light. Pinch new growth until the entire ball is totally filled in.

How to Plant a Victorian Bouquet Hanging Basket

What You'll Need

- ❑ A 10-14" wire basket prestuffed with sphagnum moss
- ❑ A 2-quart bag of potting soil
- ❑ 9 small plants (try a mix of 3 each: pink pansies, blue lobelia, and white alyssum)
- ❑ 1 tablespoon granular, slow-release fertilizer (like 14-14-14)

Fill the basket with potting soil and mix in the fertilizer in the top 1" of soil.

Plant three pansies around the rim in the top of the basket.

Victorian-style baskets can add lots of old-fashioned charm.

3 Take three alyssum and plant them around the rim between the pansies, allowing both to cascade over the rim as they grow larger.

4 Take the three lobelia plants and plant them evenly in the top middle of the basket. The wire hanger may be removed if more convenient for planting.

(Top view shown with hanger removed.)

The coleus leaves, not the flowers, add the color here.

How to Plant a Colorful Foliage Basket

What You'll Need

- ❑ A 10-14" wire basket prestuffed with sphagnum moss
- ❑ A 2-quart bag of potting soil
- ❑ 6 caladium bulbs and 6 small Boston fern plants
- ❑ 1 tablespoon granular, slow-release fertilizer (like 14-14-14)

1. Starting from 1½" down from the rim of the basket to about halfway down the side of the basket, poke three evenly spaced holes with your fingers, gently placing the caladium bulbs in the holes with the raised "eyes" protruding from the basket.

2. Gently plant three Boston ferns around the sides of the basket in between the caladium bulbs.

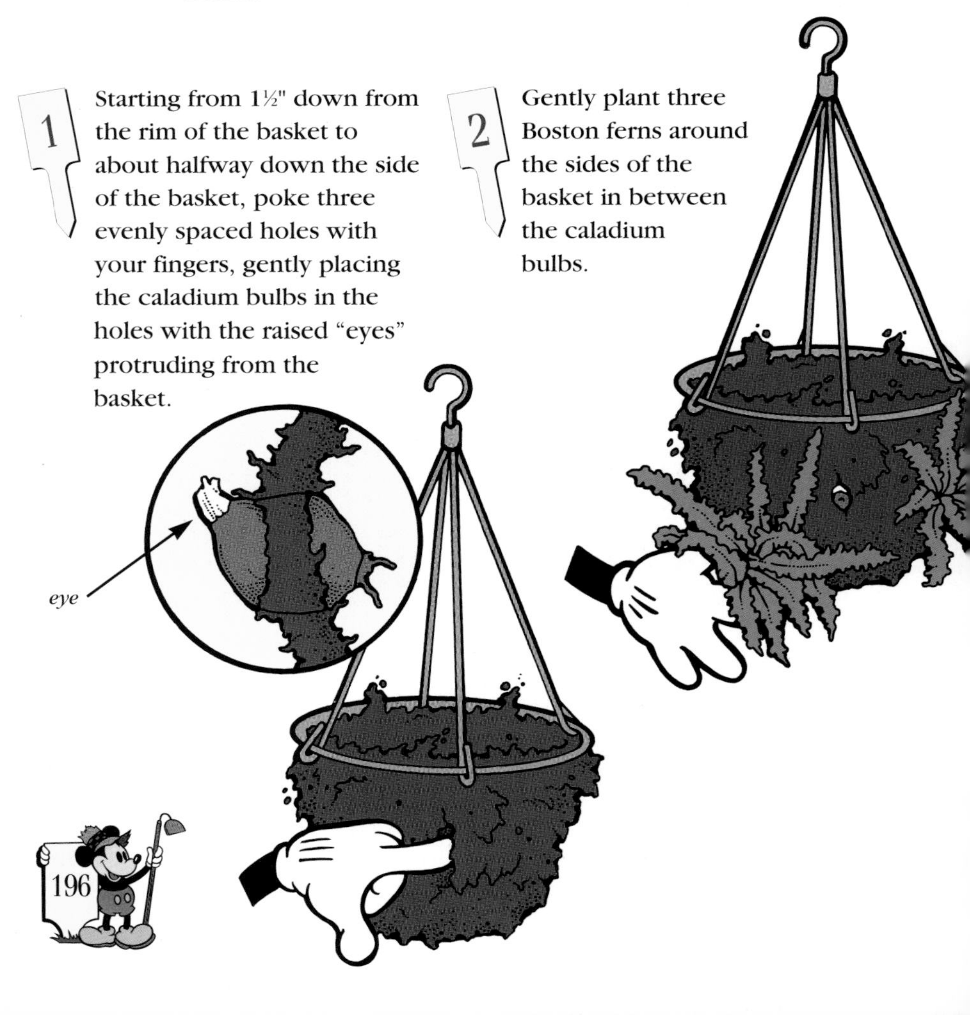

Consider unusual foliage patterns, too, when designing hanging baskets.

3 Fill the basket with potting soil and mix in the fertilizer in the top 1" of soil.

4 Evenly space the remaining three ferns and three caladium bulbs around the top. Water in thoroughly.

Hanging Basket Care

Only minor, yet consistent, maintenance is required to keep hanging baskets in tip-top shape. Immediately remove faded flower blossoms to encourage more flower growth. Prune stray shoots to retain basket shape. Fertilize weekly with a 20-20-20 water soluble fertilizer, and check daily to see if the basket needs watering. In some climate zones, hanging baskets are watered each day in the summer and every two to three days during cooler weather. Watering is a simple task if you use extra-long or curved wand watering devices. Be sure to watch for mealy bugs, spider mites, and fungus.

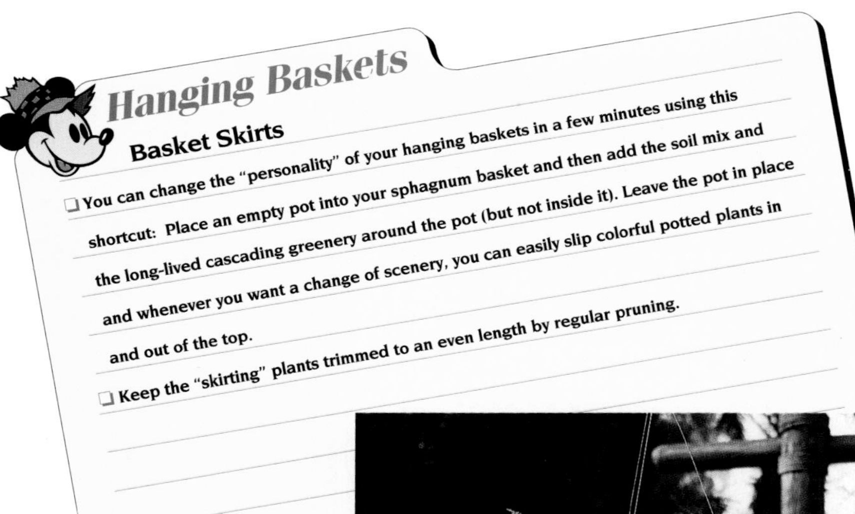

Hanging Baskets

Basket Skirts

- ❑ You can change the "personality" of your hanging baskets in a few minutes using this shortcut: Place an empty pot into your sphagnum basket and then add the soil mix and the long-lived cascading greenery around the pot (but not inside it). Leave the pot in place and whenever you want a change of scenery, you can easily slip colorful potted plants in and out of the top.
- ❑ Keep the "skirting" plants trimmed to an even length by regular pruning.

Poinsettias and ferns are paired to create a tropical-style hanging basket.

Hanging baskets high in the sky draw your eye toward Cinderella Castle in Magic Kingdom Park.

Hanging Baskets

Keys to Success

- ❑ Stuff the sphagnum tightly and keep the moss moist. Your basket may live up to two years!
- ❑ Try the "drop test." Once you've packed your basket with sphagnum moss, drop it to the floor. If it falls apart, add more moss making sure to pack it in tightly. Drop it again. If it holds together, you can be sure the basket will last through the seasons.
- ❑ When using plastic hanging baskets, remove the saucer at first to encourage good drainage. As the plants mature, replace the saucer so the soil does not dry out as quickly.
- ❑ Remember to keep the concentration of granular, slow-release fertilizer away from the crowns of young plants to prevent "fertilizer burn."

T R I V I A

- There are 151 poinsettia baskets on display during Christmas in the Magic Kingdom. If stacked one on top of another, that would reach the top of both 55-foot totem poles in the lobby of Disney's Wilderness Lodge!

- The smallest hanging baskets you'll see are at Mickey's Starland. Buildings there are scaled down to children's proportions, so the diminutive, 8" baskets are just the right size.

- The largest hanging chrysanthemum basket on view in the Walt Disney World Resort is at Journey into Imagination at EPCOT during the Thanksgiving holiday. When fully grown and watered, the three-foot-round wire and sphagnum basket weighs a scale-tipping 65 pounds.

- The first hanging baskets that ever appeared in the Magic Kingdom at Walt Disney World Resort were on Main Street, U.S.A.

- The most eclectic grouping of hanging baskets are found at Sid Cahuenga's One-of-a-Kind on Hollywood Boulevard at Disney-MGM Studios Theme Park. These baskets are purposely mismatched to mirror the eccentric nature of the shop.

- Make a stop at Frontierland in the Magic Kingdom to view baskets full of succulent plants reminiscent of Southwest deserts.

- At least 1,500 baskets are in production at any one time to maintain and replace the 650 hanging baskets on display throughout Walt Disney World Resort.

- The total number of hanging baskets produced for Walt Disney World Resort is over 13,950 per year!

Mickey and Minnie Mous wave a cheer welcome to guests visitin the Magic Kingdom Par

Rotund dancing hippos. A lumpy, bumpy sea serpent. A parade of elephants. Graceful swans and playful seals. Snow White and the Seven Dwarfs. Intricate mazes and formal hedges. Dramatic rows of gumdrop-shaped trees. Hundreds of these photogenic topiary artworks flourish throughout Walt Disney World Resort and Disneyland Park.

Roses accentuate the beauty of geometric free-form and character topiary.

Topiary gardening, the art of fashioning living plants into ornamental shapes, has been practiced for literally hundreds of years, but it wasn't until this century that it truly came to "life." Walt Disney had witnessed topiary gardening techniques in Europe and his ever-inventive mind instinctively knew there was a place for this art form in his world. The impressive talents of his film animators were combined with those of the equally talented Disneyland landscaping team to create the first living sculptures for Disneyland in 1963. The green menagerie, including Dumbo, appropriately made their auspicious debut in Fantasyland.

Topiary gardening, "Disney-style," continues to evolve. Guests in the Disney Parks today may be surprised by twirling topiary hippos, awed by a Snow White topiary dressed in striking floral attire, amused by a water-spouting topiary, or greeted by animated Mickey and Minnie topiaries waving to the crowd.

Guests visiting the Parks will find two very different styles of topiary — geometric free-form and character, and two different methods — shrub and sphagnum.

Geometric Free-form Topiary

Geometric free-form topiary is the oldest form of topiary and has been practiced throughout gardens around the world for centuries. In fact, today's home gardeners are applying free-form topiary principles by simply shaping their hedges. Over the years, Disney gardeners have been challenged by Disney Imagineers to enhance or create particular themes and moods in the landscape. To make this happen, shrubs and trees have taken on unnatural shapes to accentuate or emulate the curve of a walkway or the sharp architectural angles of a building, or to create a dramatic focal point in a particular landscape.

Topiaries create a dramatic entry into Disney's Contemporary Resort.

For example, guests visiting the Magic Kingdom will find soaring columns of dramatically sheared Japanese yews *(Podocarpus macrophyllus)* punctuating the skyline of Tomorrowland. At EPCOT, native Florida oaks are gently coerced into such unnatural shapes as cubes and pyramids, stretching even the most creative gardener's imagination in Future World. At Disneyland Park, hundreds of plants in all shapes and sizes complement the fanciful facade at It's a Small World.

A cloud-like topiary arises in front of It's a Small World *in* Disneyland Park.

Free-form topiary is relatively simple for the home gardener to design. Some imaginative shearing can transform a straight line of mature privet into a playful, snaky curve, or a tall podocarpus into puffs of clouds, or dense hedges into sharply geometric configurations.

The training of Disney topiaries is performed at the Nursery and only after they are fully mature will they make their appearance. While most are sheared freehand, sometimes special training methods are needed to create picture-perfect shapes.

Geometric shrub topiaries radiate from curvilinear architecture.

One method Disney gardeners use is attaching string lines starting at the top of a shrub and extending them out at equal angles to the ground. Using the strings as a guide, the shrub is sheared over time into a clearly defined pyramid shape. Another trick to ensure that topiary shapes stay consistent over time is to make a pipe or wooden "template" to use as a shearing guide.

Some free-form topiary features, such as mazes, ornate hedges, and other special effects involving multiple specimens, are so large or complex that they must be planned and grown as a series of smaller pieces. When the topiaries are ready for planting, they are disassembled, carefully numbered, and tagged for easier transport to their final destination. Once they reach the new location, they are carefully put back together like a huge puzzle.

Home gardeners considering adding free-form topiary to a garden plan should determine where a topiary would enhance the landscape, not block any views, and be able to grow for a long time. Patience is required because it may take several years before the topiary reaches mature size and can be shaped into the design you have in mind.

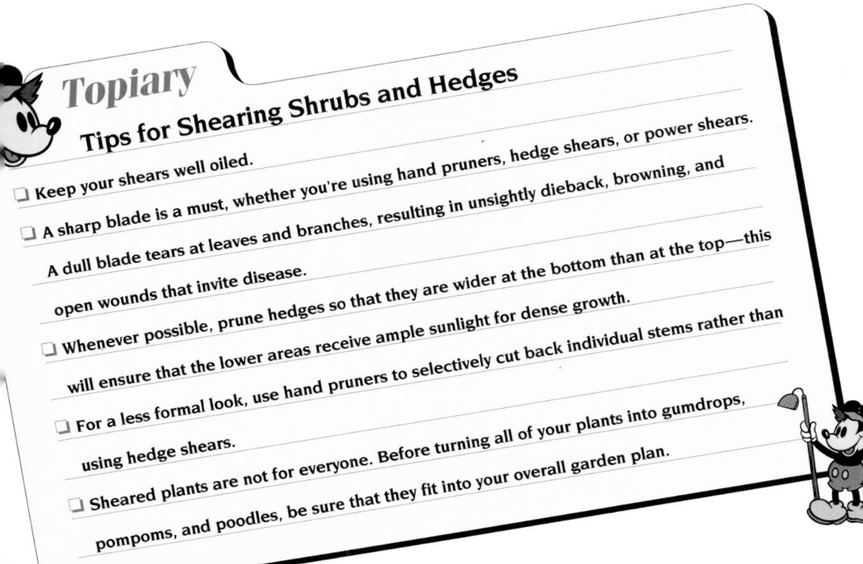

Topiary
Tips for Shearing Shrubs and Hedges

- Keep your shears well oiled.
- A sharp blade is a must, whether you're using hand pruners, hedge shears, or power shears. A dull blade tears at leaves and branches, resulting in unsightly dieback, browning, and open wounds that invite disease.
- Whenever possible, prune hedges so that they are wider at the bottom than at the top—this will ensure that the lower areas receive ample sunlight for dense growth.
- For a less formal look, use hand pruners to selectively cut back individual stems rather than using hedge shears.
- Sheared plants are not for everyone. Before turning all of your plants into gumdrops, pompoms, and poodles, be sure that they fit into your overall garden plan.

Snow White and friends skip through a field of flowers.

Character Topiary

The charm of Disney character topiary is almost irresistible. It is hard not to smile at the first recognition of a leafy green Mickey Mouse or take a second peek at a line of topiary elephants. For over a quarter century, guests from around the world have been taking photographs of their families and friends standing happily next to their favorite Disney characters all dressed in their finest greenery.

Disney character topiaries are produced in two different ways, with each method suited to meet a particular need in the Disney Parks and Resorts. The first method is referred to as "shrub character topiary" and is the most traditional of the two types. Basically a shrub planted in a large container and trained within a metal frame, shrub character topiaries are grown with the intent of becoming a permanent addition to the landscape. Aside from frequent shearings, this style of topiary requires care no different from other shrubs and trees in the landscape. Shrub topiaries, however do require considerable time to produce and due to their size and weight, are not moved about on a moment's notice. These limitations led to the development of a second technique — "sphagnum character topiary." Quick to produce, this second generation of figures has made it possible for topiaries to be used in many new and creative ways. Sphagnum topiaries are not rooted in the ground so they are easily transported from one location to the next for special events and have shown up in such surprising places as on parade floats, in convention halls, and on stages, as well as being featured in the garden. They also can be animated, accessorized with playful props, or accented with colorful plants or cut flowers.

The entire process for a Disney character topiary begins with an artist's drawing. To ensure that the design is appropriate for this unique form of sculpture, many different versions may be considered before the final pose is selected.

This sea serpent topiary creates an amusing illusion.

Next, a small scale-sized maquette (clay replica) is sculpted to make sure that the figure will look good from every angle and that the design will be effective when translated into plants — fine details are difficult to represent and are quickly lost in this form of living sculpture. Once the figure is finalized, blueprints are drawn up and full-size steel frames are constructed to match the design.

le and the Beast wear orful floral costumes.

Both types of character topiary incorporate a metal frame or skeleton. The frames are an important and necessary element for two reasons: first, the training process is hastened because the new growth can be guided through or over the frame into complex shapes (like Dumbo's trunk, for example); and second, the frame helps Disney gardeners maintain each character true to its design (in other words, Mickey always looks just like Mickey!). The frames are custom-built for each figure and are constructed differently depending on whether they will be used for shrub or sphagnum topiary.

Once the frame is complete, the Disney gardeners take over. Using the frame as a guide and taking their cue from the drawings and models, gardeners working behind the scenes begin the process of creating a living topiary.

Shrub Character Topiary

Year after year, guests visiting the Parks are most often enthralled by the whimsical shrub character topiary. With some figures in excess of 20 years old, Disney shrub topiaries are viewed as a permanent part of the landscape by guests and gardeners alike. As such, their upkeep requirements must be similar to those of the plants around them and they must be tolerant of any weather extremes that may occur. For this reason, tried and true landscape plants that are disease resistant and cold hardy are most commonly used for assured success. Only shrubs that shear well, are naturally full, and grow relatively fast are selected for this type of topiary. The three-dimensional shapes of topiaries also create shaded surfaces underneath certain areas of the characters, so the best plants will be those that are able to grow well in both shade and full sun. Plants must also adapt well to both horizontal and downward growth patterns. Younger, vigorously growing plants are better suited to topiary than older, established plants with woody trunks. Younger plants also have a greater tendency to produce new growth, branch out more readily, and respond well to shaping and pruning.

"Wild" animal topiaries front It's a Small World in Disneyland.

Some topiary figures incorporate special plants or combinations of plants to create unusual effects or even just for fun. A pink azalea in a pig makes him bloom bright pink in the spring; curly leaf ligustrum makes a llama furry; and a gray tuxedo of Texas sage adds a touch of realism to a dark green podocarpus penguin.

A wax begonia tutu encircles this roly-poly hippo's waist.

A procession of pachyderms marches toward Magic Kingdom Park.

The frames used for shrub topiary serve only as a guide for training and pruning. They are lightweight and do not support any weight other than the frame itself. The shrubs are planted where the frame comes in contact with the soil. If the figure has four legs, for example, each leg gets its own plant. After the shrubs are in position, the frame is carefully placed over them and securely situated into the soil. Finally, the plants are mulched and watered in. As the plant fills the frame it is gently coaxed into shape by tying to conform to the unusual pattern of growth to fill in wings, tails, trunks, and all sorts of odd-shaped bits and pieces. The frame is no less than 4" in diameter at any point to allow for growth and to avoid damaging the bark.

As the shrub topiaries grow, they are clipped every week during their growing season and every two weeks the rest of the year. Disney topiary gardeners also prune to remove unnecessary branches and to prevent woody trunks from showing. They're weeded, watered, and fertilized monthly with a high-nitrogen fertilizer, too. Once the figures can be pruned at a distance 3" from the metal frame and the frame is hidden completely, they have reached maturity and are ready for display.

Shrub topiaries are planted in large, specially constructed wooden boxes with removable sides. When the topiary is

ready to take its place, a planting hole slightly larger than the box is dug at the final destination. The box is lowered in the hole and the sides are removed. The biodegradable bottom, however, stays in place to minimize transplant shock.

Shrub character topiaries can take from three to 10 years for completion, depending on the size and complexity of the figure. For example, Figment, who is only 5½' tall, may take only three years to complete, while Pete's dragon Elliot, who from head to tail is over 14' long, may take 10 years or more until ready to take its place.

A camel shrub topiary nestles in an oasis of marigolds.

Topiary

Common Shrub Topiary Plants

Australian Brush Cherry (*Syzygium paniculatum*), **Azalea** (*Rhododendron cvs.*)

Burford Holly (*Ilex cornuta* 'Burfordii'), **Cherry Laurel** (*Prunus caroliniana*)

Dwarf Myrtle (*Myrtus communis* 'Compacta'), **Fern Pine** (*Podocarpus gracilior*)

Firethorn (*Pyracantha coccinea*), **Japanese Boxwood** (*Buxus microphylla japonica*)

Japanese Privet (*Ligustrum japonicum*), **Japanese Yew** (*Podocarpus macrophyllus*)

Olive (*Olea europaea*), **Sylvester Juniper** (*Juniperus chinensis* 'Sylvestris')

Yaupon Holly (*Ilex vomitoria*)

Rule of Green Thumb: Any evergreen, fine-textured plant that shears well is a good candidate for shrub topiary.

The Other Small, Small World: Storybook Land

Guests sailing along on the Storybook Land Canal Boats attraction at Disneyland Park are often stunned when they realize everything in the incredibly tiny landscape is alive and growing! In Storybook Land, familiar scenes from classic Disney films, including *Cinderella* and *Aladdin*, are brought to life in perfect miniature scale: one inch is equal to one foot.

To enhance the diminutive effect, the minute villages and buildings are ingeniously landscaped with proportionally sized plants and flowers. Disney landscapers select plants with a leaf size of little more than 1/4" and further restrict growth by planting many specimens in containers. A "magical potion" is also added to the trees and shrubs to likewise limit plant size.

Horticultural creativity is evident everywhere in Storybook Land. A 3'-tall Japanese boxwood topiary, with gnarled trunk, was shaped and pruned to represent the oak tree where Alice entered the Rabbit Hole in Wonderland. An old grapevine was uprooted and turned upside down to create the "terribly tortured snag" in front of Ratty's home from *Wind in the Willows.*

Next to Geppetto's shop in Pinocchio's Village, a 20-year-old cypress tree stands scarcely 18" tall and *Liquidambar orientalis* bonsai accent the wee setting. Scaled-down, 25-year-old forest pines shelter Snow White's cottage. In the London Park, a Lilliputian weeping willow-type tree is actually an old, stunted *Pittosporum phillyraeoides* and the soft-looking grass is really Irish moss. A cruise through Storybook Land is truly a glimpse of landscaping artistry at its finest.

Topiary

Mickey's Favorite Plants for Shrub Topiary

	DISNEYLAND	WALT DISNEY WORLD
Australian Brush Cherry (*Syzygium paniculatum*)	●	
Firethorn (*Pyracantha coccinea*)	●	●
Japanese Yew (*Podocarpus macrophyllus*)	●	●
Olive (*Olea europaea*)	●	
Yaupon Holly (*Ilex vomitoria*)		●

How to Make a Spiral Shrub Topiary

What You'll Need

- ❑ A young, evergreen shrub, about 6' high and 2' wide, with a straight, single trunk that serves as a strong central leader. A shrubby, upright juniper (such as *Juniperus chinensis 'Robusta Green'*) or similar plant is a good choice.
- ❑ A roll of 1"-wide ribbon
- ❑ Hand pruners
- ❑ Hedge shears
- ❑ A good eye and lots of patience!

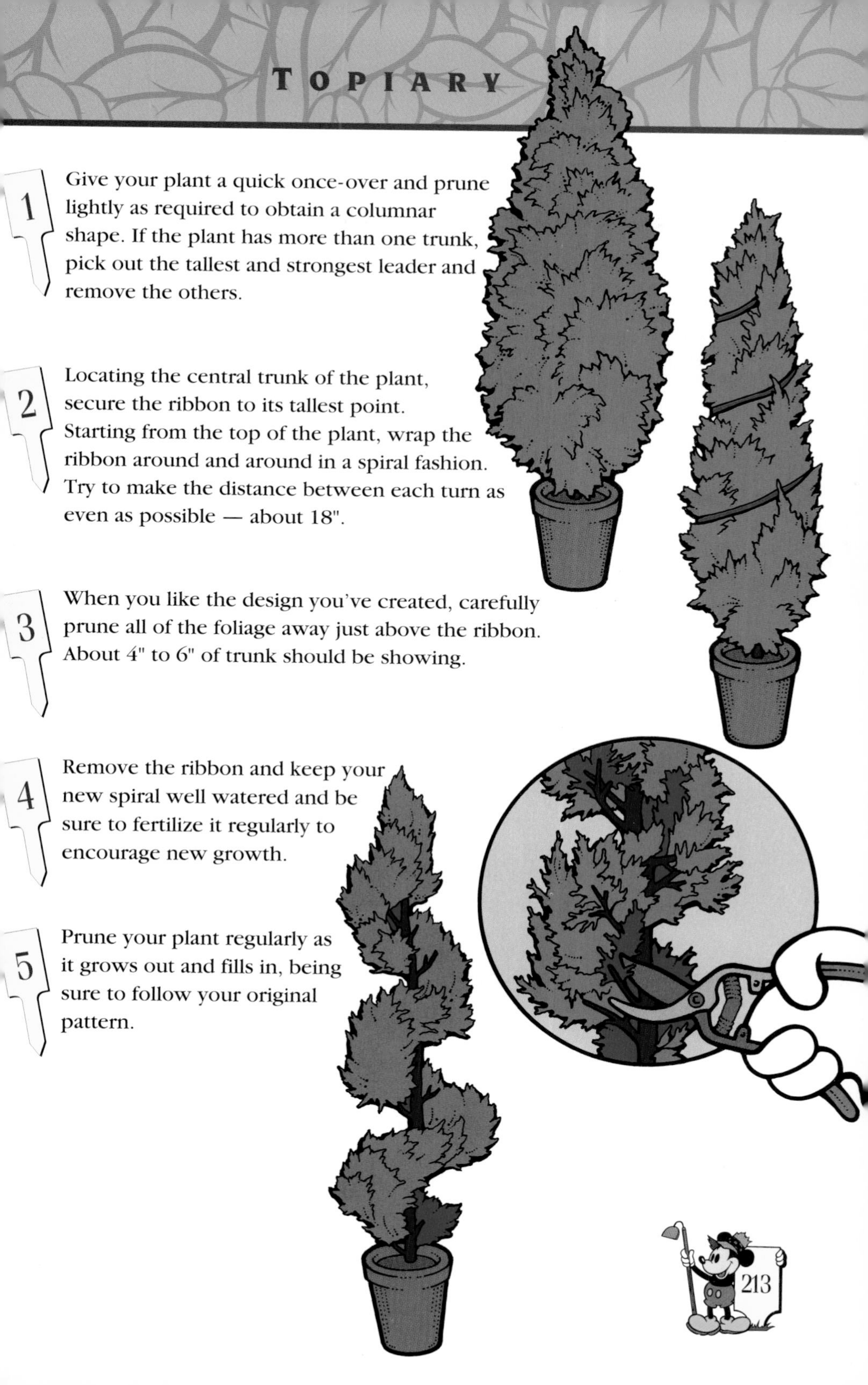

1. Give your plant a quick once-over and prune lightly as required to obtain a columnar shape. If the plant has more than one trunk, pick out the tallest and strongest leader and remove the others.

2. Locating the central trunk of the plant, secure the ribbon to its tallest point. Starting from the top of the plant, wrap the ribbon around and around in a spiral fashion. Try to make the distance between each turn as even as possible — about 18".

3. When you like the design you've created, carefully prune all of the foliage away just above the ribbon. About 4" to 6" of trunk should be showing.

4. Remove the ribbon and keep your new spiral well watered and be sure to fertilize it regularly to encourage new growth.

5. Prune your plant regularly as it grows out and fills in, being sure to follow your original pattern.

Sphagnum Character Topiary

The idea for sphagnum topiary was born out of necessity. There was a need for character topiary that was easy to make, portable for special events, and didn't require the long production time the shrub topiaries call for. So, an entirely different technique was devised to create a sphagnum topiary character. In its simplest form, a sphagnum topiary is a steel frame stuffed with sphagnum moss which is then planted with vines.

From outward appearances, a frame for sphagnum topiary looks very similar to those used for shrub topiary. The similarity stops there, though. A sphagnum topiary frame actually has structural supports in the middle to handle the heavy weight of the moist sphagnum and incorporates a sturdy stand to make transporting the figure simpler. Often, special lifting hooks or forklift sleeves are designed into the frame to further simplify transporting sphagnum figures. In preparation for planting, the frame is carefully wrapped with chicken wire and then stuffed with unmilled sphagnum moss. To lighten the weight, some of the larger topiary figures have Styrofoam™ "filler" in their centers.

Crocodile and hippo characters from Fantasia *stand poised near* Spaceship Earth.

After the frame is stuffed, small plants known as "plugs" are planted into the sphagnum. Creeping vines, like English ivy cultivars or creeping fig, are secured to the form with florist or hair pins. While most figures have a coat of solid green, plants with colorful foliage, like wax begonias can also be used to add a touch of brilliant contrast. The figures are produced in a greenhouse which ensures optimum growing conditions year 'round. The key to how long the process takes is how tightly the plugs are spaced. Disney gardeners plant six to nine plugs per square foot. With persistent tender loving care a sphagnum topiary can be ready to show in three months or less.

Sphagnum topiaries require daily care and are not for the casual gardener. The plants are inserted directly into the sphagnum with little or no soil, so receiving the proper amount of water is critical to their survival. Delicate extremities, like Mickey's fingers and Dumbo's trunk, dry out first and need to be checked carefully each day. In comparison, lower body parts, especially those in shaded locations, tend to stay moist. A delicate balance in watering is the key to success.

Sphagnum topiaries are also fertilized once a week with a water-soluble 20-20-20 fertilizer (at half the rate recommended on the label) using a hose-end proportioner sprayer. Routine maintenance includes keeping stray growth in line by pinning the vines to the figure and pruning to encourage dense growth and rapid coverage.

"Portable" sphagnum topiaries are frequently used for special events.

A topiary bison keeps watch over Disney's Wilderness Lodge.

Mickey welcomes guests at Disney-MGM Studios Theme Park.

In the cooler months, depending upon the plant used, a topiary may need some additional care to protect it from the cold. An ivy topiary may survive freezing temperatures, but most should be either brought inside to a sunny location or otherwise protected from the elements outside. Disney gardeners go to great measures to keep their topiaries healthy. Sometimes heaters are placed around them, occasionally they are covered with insulating wraps, and in the coldest weather, a tent of lightweight fabric is placed over them with a heater installed inside.

In addition to all of this regular care, sphagnum figures receive a complete "make over" every three to five years to keep them looking their best. At this time, the figure is revitalized, the old moss replaced with new, and replanted.

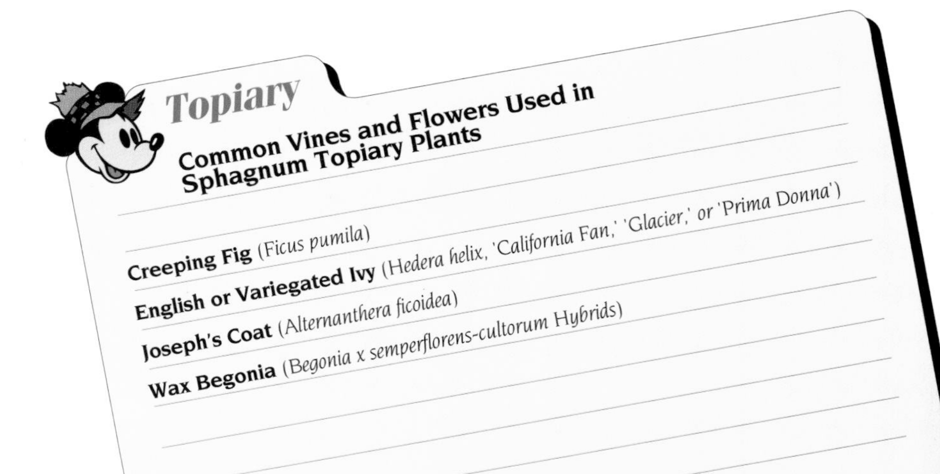

Topiary

Common Vines and Flowers Used in Sphagnum Topiary Plants

Creeping Fig (*Ficus pumila*)
English or Variegated Ivy (*Hedera helix*, 'California Fan,' 'Glacier,' or 'Prima Donna')
Joseph's Coat (*Alternanthera ficoidea*)
Wax Begonia (*Begonia x semperflorens-cultorum Hybrids*)

How to Make a Tabletop Topiary

What You'll Need

- ❑ A prefabricated wire frame
  (Many shapes and styles are available. Check your local garden center or gardening magazines for sources.)
- ❑ Unmilled sphagnum moss
- ❑ Florist pins
  (Hair pins will do, too!)
- ❑ A roll of medium-weight fishing line
- ❑ Several small plants or rooted cuttings
  (Creeping fig or English ivy are good choices.)
- ❑ A bucket
- ❑ Scissors
- ❑ Hand pruners
- ❑ Gloves

Tabletop topiaries are fun and quick to create.

Add a tabletop topiary to a container of low-growing plants.

Moisten several handfuls of sphagnum moss by immersing it in a bucket of water (be sure to wear gloves when handling sphagnum moss).

2

Carefully begin stuffing the moss into the frame, starting with extremities such as the head, arms, legs, or tail.

3

As you finish a section, tie the end of your fishing line to the frame and tightly wrap the moss, following the contours of the frame. Don't worry if your topiary looks a little "shaggy" at this point — a "haircut" with a pair of scissors will take care of that.

Continue stuffing the body with moss. Position your plant in the moss on the surfac of your figure (larger frames will cover more quickly if several plants are used).

5 Being sure that your plant is comfortably tucked in with moss, finish wrapping the figure with fishing line, and give the moss a final trim.

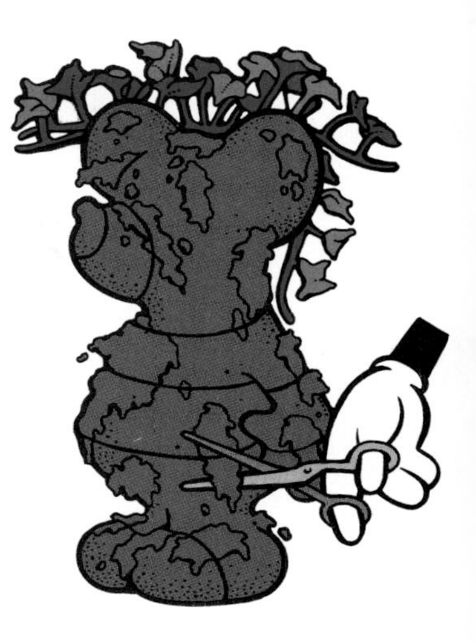

6 Carefully pin each individual vine of your plant to the moss (directing long runners up necks or tails will speed coverage).

7 Keep your tabletop topiary healthy by placing it on a patio or porch in bright light. Keep your figure moist and use a liquid fertilizer regularly. Trim and pin new growth until the entire form is covered.

TRIVIA

- At Walt Disney World Resort, over 60 character topiary figures are always in production behind the scenes in an area known amusingly as the "Chlorophyll Zoo."

- Construction schedules were too tight to grow all the topiary needed for the 1971 Walt Disney World Resort opening, so Disneyland came to the rescue, providing 12 topiaries just in time for the big day.

- In 1987, Disney gardeners in Florida had the opportunity to return the favor. Four topiary elephants "packed their trunks" for a 2,429-mile journey to Disneyland Park for a starring role alongside Dumbo in Fantasyland.

- Nearly 10,000 creeping fig *(Ficus pumila)* plants were required to prepare 14 topiary figures for the "Fantasia Topiary Garden," created especially for the 1994 Epcot International Flower & Garden Festival.

- Pete's dragon Elliot is the largest shrub character topiary at Walt Disney World Resort. The *Podocarpus macrophyllus* topiary was grown and trained for 10 years and stands over 10' tall and 14' long from head to tail.

- The oldest topiaries made their premiere in 1963 in Disneyland Park. There were a total of 24, including a waltzing hippo, a poodle, a pig, bears, elephants, seals, and giraffes. In 1966, they were permanently planted in the forecourt of It's a Small World in Fantasyland.

- Nearly 2,525 yellow, blue, red, and white carnations are attached by hand to create the colorful attire for the Snow White floral topiary at Walt Disney World Resort.

- Seventeen topiaries went on a rare road trip for the 1993 Flower and Garden Show in New York City. Mickey and Minnie Mouse, Donald Duck, Pluto, Snow White and the seven dwarfs and other familiar characters traveled from Walt Disney World Resort in Florida for display.

Parterre Gardens

The famous "Mickey Flora greets million of visitors to Disneyland Park.

Nearly everyone has seen aerial photographs of the vast and elegantly designed parterre gardens surrounding French castles. Their impressive swirl patterns and bold geometric shapes are formed by densely spaced bushes, perfectly manicured lawns, elaborately trimmed trees, and abundant flower blossoms. The spectacular effect is almost like intricate embroidery. Most people obviously don't have the space, funds, time, or interest in creating a parterre garden of such massive size, but it can be loads of fun and visually rewarding to experiment on a small scale. Dedication is the key!

"Parterre" is a French word meaning "on the ground." In its simplest definition, parterre refers to any ornamental arrangement of flowerbeds and pathways in different shapes and sizes that create pictures on the earth. The designs are usually best viewed from a high vantage point or from a distance. For this reason, many parterre gardens are built on a gentle slope or in a position where viewing is done from afar. For example, at Disneyland Park there are complex parterre designs along the sloped gardens framing It's a Small World.

Creative designs and colorful plant combinations are naturals in parterre gardens.

Mickey Mouse's flowery face greeting visitors to Disneyland Park is the most universally recognized parterre garden in the world. The "Mickey Floral" debuted at the opening of Disneyland Park in 1955 and immediately became a favorite location of shutterbugs from around the world.

A floral Mickey celebrates the Golden Age of Hollywood in Disney-MGM Studios Theme Park.

Subsequently, Mickey Florals bloomed at the Magic Kingdom Park at Walt Disney World Resort, Disney-MGM Studios Theme Park, Tokyo Disneyland, and at Disneyland Paris as well. Each of the five Mickey portraits is distinctly different. The Disneyland Park Mickey originally represented the 1950s cartoon style of that period, but was later revamped into a more detailed, updated Mickey. The Mickey at the Magic Kingdom Park sports a '70s look, and Mickey at Tokyo Disneyland is a stylized '80s version. The parterre at Disney-MGM Studios Theme Park is a 1940s era Mickey and the Disneyland Paris Mickey is described as a "Happy Mickey," and sports one ear larger than the other.

Disney gardeners have created and perfected many of their own parterre gardening techniques over the years. The design of a Disney garden dictates what kind of planting methods are employed. For example, sometimes Fiberglas™ forms (called benderboards) are installed in permanent gardens that are regularly

planted with annuals. Other times, headerboards made of 2" x 4" wood are used for large lawn areas bordered by perennials where no curved lines are needed. Sometimes large grids of a design are constructed for areas of up to 15' x 15'. The grid is carefully placed on the prepared soil and the outline traced with powdered chalk from the blueprints to ensure consistency from planting to planting. The parterre garden in front of France in EPCOT is a model of this type of template planting.

A brilliant floral pattern draws visitors to Spaceship Earth in EPCOT.

The Magic Kingdom Mickey Mouse Floral

The smiling floral face of Mickey Mouse has welcomed over one *billion* guests at the entrance to the Magic Kingdom Park since 1971. As the Walt Disney World Railroad chugs by in the background, the scenario is reminiscent of turn-of-the-century America at a time when people often traveled by train.

'ckey sports a bold, new look every season.

Pioneers settling the western frontier had little time for leisurely gardening during the 1800s. However, they sometimes lavished what little extra time they had on beautifying the railroad station grounds. Formal beds of colorful flowers (sometimes spelling out the town's name) signaled their hospitality to daily visitors.

The Magic Kingdom Mickey Mouse Floral is planted several times a year with approximately 2,000 4" bedding plants. It takes a team of gardeners seven to eight hours to replant each time. Park guests like to view the Mickey parterre up close, too, so 25 hours per week is spent carefully trimming the outlining hedges and deadheading flowers.

The EPCOT symbol lends itself to an intricate parterre garden design.

Planning Your Parterre Garden

Disney parterre gardens are created to enhance the architectural style of surrounding themed areas, embellish walkways, beautify seating areas, and contribute to the overall appearance and viewing pleasure of the terrain. Think about these concepts when planning your own parterre garden.

Walk around in your yard. View your environment from across the street, from upstairs and downstairs windows, from the back porch, and anywhere you can get a picture of the yard as a whole. Start sketching scale drawings of your favorite ideas based on what you think would work in your own landscape. As you plant your garden, don't forget to make notes on your sketches indicating what you planted, how long the garden lasted, and what pointers you want to remember for next time. And most importantly, TAKE PICTURES!

A bit of Hollywood whimsy stars in Disney-MGM Studios Theme Park.

This panoramic parterre is in Storybook Land in Disneyland Park.

Little Mouse on the Prairie

To uniquely commemorate Mickey Mouse's 60th birthday in 1988, a one-mile-square cornfield in the middle of the United States was planted into a very distinctive shape. An accommodating farmer in Sheffield, Iowa (population 1,200) agreed to plant the 520 acres, outlining Mickey's head with green cornstalks on a contrasting background of golden-brown oats.

The massive field was three times the size of Disneyland, including the parking lot! Air travelers flying from New York to San Francisco or Houston to Minneapolis could gaze out at 35,000 feet and instantly recognize the image.

An aerial view of "Kernel Mickey" delighted air travelers in 1988.

Later, the fall harvest produced 35,000 bushels of Mickey corn. Some of the corn fed the farmer's 3,000 hogs and the rest went to market. E-I-E-I-OOOOOH!

Parterre

Parterre Garden Tips

- Use compact annuals with clear, bright colors.
- For easier viewing, plant your parterre in a raised, slanted bed.
- Plants with colorful foliage, like dusty miller, alternanthera, and coleus, work well in parterre gardens.
- Begonias are favorites for Disney parterre gardens because of their compact growing habit.

How to Make a Parterre Flower Bed

What You'll Need

- ❑ A sketch of your design (directions are for a 10' x 10' area)
- ❑ 4 three cubic yard-sized bags of soil amendments like peat or manure
- ❑ 10 lbs. gypsum
- ❑ 2 lbs. complete fertilizer
- ❑ Shovel or rototiller
- ❑ Rake
- ❑ 200 plants (space 6" apart)
- ❑ Headerboards or benderboards, if desired

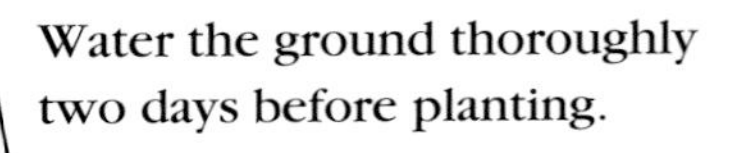

1 Water the ground thoroughly two days before planting.

2 Turn the soil over as deeply as possible with a shovel or rototiller if you're planning a large parterre. Be sure to dig down at least 6" for adequate drainage. Break up any soil clumps.

3 Spread any necessary soil amendments evenly over the s and then sprinkle the gypsum and fertilizer over that. Mix the soil completely by repeating th digging and turning process.

4 Rake the soil so it's level, being careful not to compact the soil by walking across it too much. Remove any remaining clumps or rocks on the soil surface.

5 Arrange the headerboards or benderboards according to your design and press them flush into the ground. Water thoroughly letting the soil settle.

6 Begin planting.

Note: If you want to create a very simple parterre garden without the headerboards or benderboards, just trace the pattern into the prepared soil with a stick and then plant! Disney gardeners sometimes put lime or chalk in a plastic, ketchup-type squeeze bottle with a tip on it to "draw" their designs.

EPCOT Fleur-de-lis Garden

Gracing a grassy hill near France in EPCOT is a beautiful "fleur-de-lis" parterre garden. Translated from French, fleur-de-lis means "flower of the lily." The name refers to the iris-like design the kings of France used in the creation of their heraldry.

This visual favorite is best viewed from the bridge or International Gateway in EPCOT.

Heraldry is the practice of devising insignias (family crests, emblems, and coats of arms) to distinguish individual families and to authenticate official documents.

Legend tells us that the fleur-de-lis was originally used in heraldry around 500 A.D. after an angel reputedly gave Louis I an iris for accepting Christianity. In 1376, Charles V chose three fleur-de-lis as his coat of arms.

The landscape design objective facing Disney gardeners in the France showcase was to complement the French-style architecture, streets, and fountains, and enhance the illusion of a springtime garden in seventeenth century Paris. The complex fleur-de-lis pattern was chosen not only for its beauty, but for its importance in French history as well.

The legendary fleur-de-lis at France in EPCOT.

Common Plants for Parterre Gardens

African Boxwood
**Alternanthera ficoidea* (italic, marked *)
Alyssum
*Japanese Boxwood
Chrysanthemum
Coleus
Compact Eugenia
Dusty Miller
Dwarf Holly
Dwarf Myrtle
Euonymus
Geranium
Herbs
Ilex vomitoria 'Schilling'
Impatiens
Pansy
Petunia
Roses
Wax Begonia

**Most commonly used as the outline pattern for the bedges.*

A geometric floral is a colorful accent around a flagpole in Disney's Contemporary Resort.

TRIVIA

- Nearly 6,000 annuals are planted at least four times a year in Disneyland Park to keep the Mickey Mouse Floral parterre in tip-top shape.

- The "Le Nôtre Garden" in front of France in EPCOT is a miniature example of *parterre de broderie* (embroidered parterre design). The design is patterned after and named for its designer, André Le Nôtre, the leading garden designer for Louis XIV in the sixteenth century.

- At United Kingdom in EPCOT, gardeners mix red, yellow, and white miniature roses to add color to the boxwood parterre gardens.

ORIENTAL GARDENS
Herb Gardens
HUMMINGBIRD GARDENS
DESERT GARDENS
TROPICAL Gardens
Cottage Gardens
Butterfly GARDENS
Fragrance
PRAIRIE

Pink cosmos help set the theme in thi[s] cottage garde[n]

Creating a theme garden is often a labor of love or the fulfillment of a dream. Sometimes it reflects a gardener's interest in a particular era in history, such as the Victorian age, Colonial days, or Shakespearean time. Occasionally there is a cultural influence that results in an Oriental themed garden or early American pioneer garden. Perhaps lingering memories of a pleasant vacation to a tropical paradise, mountain retreat, or European countryside urge a gardener to recreate a landscape. Theme gardens can be a place very close to home where you can "get away from it all."

Theme gardens can also be showcases for particular types of plants, like roses, cacti, orchids, wildflowers, or herbs. They can be designed to entice wildlife or provide a refuge filled with heavenly fragrances. Theme gardens allow you to personalize your landscape, focus on special interests, and reproduce a particular mood, or geographic, historical, or cultural place or period.

***A futuristic garden setting fronts Universe of Energy in* EPCOT.**

Disney gardeners create theme gardens primarily to "set a stage." Each landscape is carefully designed to coordinate flowers, trees, shrubs, grasses, and garden accents to enhance and complement whatever the desired mood, architectural design, or cultural feeling is desired in a particular area. Nothing is randomly planted, every plant has its own special purpose.

This concept of theming was very important to Walt Disney even in the early 1950s when he was planning Disneyland. He knew that every element of a setting was integral to telling the "story," whether it was the tropical forest created for the Jungle Cruise, the futuristic gardens of Tomorrowland, or the Old West desert landscaping for Frontierland. The idea was to convey the feeling that you've been transported to another time or place.

This philosophy and commitment to theme gardens matching a location has been carried on and improved upon year after year in all the Walt Disney Theme Parks and Resorts. Even the casual, unplanned look of the cottage garden at United Kingdom in EPCOT is carefully choreographed down to the last detail. Likewise, the palm-lined Hollywood Boulevard in Disney-MGM Studios Theme Park and the Great American wilderness forest of Critter Country in Disneyland Park were researched, designed, and created to present a specific theme.

Planning Your Theme Garden

Your inspiration can come from many sources. Review books and magazines featuring theme gardens, travel, garden history, and specific geographic locations. Visit botanical gardens, join clubs specializing in gardens that interest you, and take a cue from your own garden setting. Determine what type of theme garden would be appropriate in your existing landscape and how it might complement the architecture of your home. Ask yourself what function you want your themed garden to perform. Do you want a quiet place for reflection? A secluded spot to watch hummingbirds and butterflies? A garden to accent your home's architectural style?

Cacti and drought-tolerant plants accentuate the desert theme at Big Thunder Mountain in Magic Kingdom Park.

Once you've decided on your theme, begin your research and start making your plant selections. Disney gardeners prefer authenticity in the plants they select, and have often gone to great lengths to procure their perfect specimens.

Sometimes "stand-in" plants are substituted when the real thing won't grow in an environment it's unaccustomed to. Many plants have convincing look-alikes that will thrive in your location and recreate the theme you're trying to convey. Ask your local agricultural extension agent or nursery personnel for their recommendations.

Disney Theme Gardens

Nowhere in Walt Disney World Theme Parks and Resorts do theme gardens play a more noticeable role than around the World Showcase in EPCOT. These landscapes are graphic examples of how theme gardens can make a significant impact on the overall atmosphere and enjoyment of a setting. A stroll around the World Showcase lagoon takes you from a Mexican jungle, to a Norwegian woodland, past a tranquil Chinese meditation pond, to a Bavarian "platz" complete with geranium-filled window boxes, to an Italian piazza decorated with terra-cotta pots brimming with flowers against a soaring Italian cypress backdrop. Further on, you'll pass a red, white, and blue All-American garden, a serene Japanese rock garden, an arid Moroccan oasis, a French boulevard lined with sycamore and crape myrtle, an English country garden, the majestic, pine-topped mountains of Canada and the formal Victoria Garden.

Geranium-filled window boxes and decorative painting highlight the Bavarian-themed street at Germany in EPCOT.

Terra-cotta pots and statuary decorate this piazza at Italy in EPCOT.

Throughout Future World in EPCOT, the landscapes reflect the modern lines of the sleekly designed architecture. Flowers are planted in sharply angled or wide, curving beds of solid color, emphasizing a bold, contemporary theme.

Outside Journey into Imagination, plants are playfully combined with "leap frog" fountains that lightly splash unwary guests and the impish children who wait for the watery spray to hit them. Chinese evergreens and Japanese yew are sculptured into unique, unnatural shapes underscoring the futuristic environment. Live oak trees are sheared to parallel the roofline of Universe of Energy in EPCOT, adding to the precisely contrived appearance of the environment.

"Spooky" landscaping conjures a "dreadful" feeling at The Haunted Mansion in Magic Kingdom Park.

In Disneyland Park and Magic Kingdom Park, smiling Mickey parterre gardens welcome guests, just as parterres greeted weary travelers reaching train stations at the turn of the century. Old-fashioned American charm abounds on Main Street, U.S.A. The Wild West comes alive in Frontierland. Exotic jungles envelop Adventureland. Gardens of whimsy add charm to Fantasyland, Mickey's Toontown, and Mickey's Starland. Geometric plantings emphasize the futuristic look of Tomorrowland.

Lush palm trees provide island appeal at Disney's Caribbean Beach Resort.

In Disneyland Park, twisted, tortured-looking plants in a variety of gloomy colors surround The Haunted Mansion giving it that appropriately scary atmosphere. Large trees, like weeping blue juniper and magnolia, cast spooky shadows on the lawns and Medusa's Head plants grow in urns topping fence columns.

Theme gardens play leading roles in Disney-MGM Studios Theme Park, too. From a glamorous Hollywood panorama, through the urban setting of New York Street, to the eerie grounds of The Twilight Zone Tower of Terror™, the specialized landscapes bring a sense of realism to each location.

Extensive landscaping is keyed to the theme of each Disney Resort. Disney's Wilderness Lodge, for example, features natural-looking vegetation reminiscent of the Pacific Northwest and life-sized topiary buffalo.

Disney's Polynesian Resort is landscaped to resemble the lush and tropical isles of the South Seas.

The New England seaside landscape is represented at Disney's Yacht and Beach Club Resorts and a peaceful island atmosphere surrounds Disney's Caribbean Beach Resort.

Disney's Dixie Landings Resort takes guests back to Mississippi steamboating days, with stately mansions and bayou houses planted with a Southern charm.

Disney's Port Orleans Resort festively showcases the excitement of the Mardi Gras and the romance of the French Quarter with a colorful Cajun landscape.

Palms and scrub plantings imitate a Hollywood Hills feeling at Disney-MGM Studios Theme Park.

The Twilight Zone Tower of Terror™ Themed Landscape

Disney-MGM Studios Theme Park is home to the "long-abandoned, yet once glamorous" 13-story Hollywood Tower Hotel. Guests "checking in" to the attraction take a terrifying elevator plunge on The Twilight Zone Tower of Terror that lies within. As the storyline goes, the hotel enjoyed a star-filled heyday in the 1930s, complete with elegant accommodations and formal gardens surrounding the property. Today, after "years of neglect," the eerie landscape helps set the spooky stage for the supernatural thrills awaiting inside. On the approach to the ominous hotel, the landscape is reminiscent of California's Hollywood Hills and takes on a chaparral look. As guests wander up the curved driveway entrance to the hotel, they pass billboard advertisements typical of the 1930s surrounded by scrub plantings.

The hotel's patio features overgrown azalea hedges that create a maze-like setting. The "original" formal elements are still preserved, yet appear weathered. Antique plant labels and old, broken statuary with patches of "weeds" rest among the shrubs (azaleas, African iris, and Indian hawthorn). "Dead" oak trees, heavily laden with Spanish moss, reinforce the unsettling mood of the area.

The exit courtyard repeats the Spanish Revival theme of the hotel with arbors of cascading bougainvillea. Palm trees dot the entire landscape and bougainvillea spill out of ornate urns and planters on the porte-cochère. Interestingly, this "abandoned" look actually requires a great deal of maintenance.

Oriental Gardens

Chinese and Japanese gardens share many similarities, but are actually very different from one another in their design. Both styles have common elements such as water and rocks, and both celebrate nature by "painting a picture" utilizing the surrounding landscape and creating the effect of gardens within gardens.

Chinese Gardens

Chinese gardens are traditionally "passive," still, and yet complex, filled with symbolic imagery, allusion, and a sense of reverence for nature. Gardens in China are used for celebrations, family commemorations, peaceful refuge, and to simply commune with nature. Water, typically a reflecting pond, is used to mirror the beauty of the landscape and surrounding architecture. This type of garden offers a serene haven for meditation and, in China, thoughtful planning always goes into selecting the perfect location. Many Chinese people consider it a guarantee of happiness to plan a garden facing south and often do so.

A solitary, gnarled tree sometimes dominates the scene in a Chinese garden. The tree's twisted and ancient appearance may be so unearthly that a new standard of beauty emerges. Your mind's eye is forced into seeing nature with a new clarity and reverence.

A wildly distorted tree becomes an oddly beautiful focal point at China in EPCOT.

Floating planters of chrysanthemums and ferns grace the tranquil pond at China *in* EPCOT.

Central China's mountains, with their incredibly stunning peaks, greatly influenced the Chinese ideal of natural beauty. Weirdly eroded rocks in contorted shapes, suggesting mountains, are predominant attributes in nearly every Chinese garden. Some devoted gardeners even employ "rock brokers" to search out the ultimate rocks for their gardens. Prized rocks are often lichen-covered and weathered, and considered to be more "expressive." Centuries ago, fine rocks were regarded as prestigious objects to be treasured and admired.

The gardens at China in EPCOT are inspired by man's efforts to achieve harmony between self and nature. The gardens are passive and soothing.

Paths and bridges lead guests on a fascinating stroll where every vista offers beautiful visual rewards. Each garden setting takes on its own "still-life" quality.

Ancient-looking rocks are prized additions to Chinese gardens.

A placid meditation pond reflects the surrounding rocks, plants, and the three-tiered Hall of Prayer for Good Harvests. The boldly painted, gold-accented building is modeled after the famous landmark at the Temple of Heaven Park near Beijing.

Trees and shrubs with twisted branches, like corkscrew willow, weeping mulberry, and Harry Lauder's walking stick, contribute to the theme of antiquity. Dramatic evening lighting is mirrored on the still water, accenting the landscaping and the large, weathered rocks jutting from the water.

The Chinese word for landscape is "shanshui," which literally means "mountains and water." The geography of China helps us to understand the origin of the Chinese garden — 85% of China is dominated by mountains. Hence, the importance of rocks and water in the garden.

Japanese Gardens

Japanese gardens are typically "active," simple, orderly, natural, and yet controlled in appearance. Often, they are small-scale versions of nature at its finest and feature natural materials like bamboo and unpainted wood for fences and bridges. Japanese gardens are usually more colorful than Chinese gardens and sometimes the look is accentuated with "happy-colored" flowers of pink and white.

Simplicity is the key in this "active" garden setting at Japan in EPCOT.

Sound in the garden is also important. The clattering of bamboo stalks in the wind, the hollow "clack" of a handcrafted deer scare, the bubbling, gurgling, and splashing of water, are all key elements in a Japanese garden. Ponds, stocked with colorful koi fish, are also typical. Shrubs and other plants are usually arranged in groups of 1, 3, 5, or 7 (considered lucky numbers) and are often pruned into specific shapes. Disney gardeners prune and trim some of their bushes into fluffy cloud shapes.

Bonsai plants are grown in small containers and meticulously pruned to resemble the dignity and perfection of ancient trees and shrubs in miniature. They can live for hundreds of years and are prized possessions in Japan, passed through generations of families. Usually these plants are grown in containers indoors, but somewhat larger versions of bonsai are frequently added to the outdoor Japanese garden landscape.

A solitary bonsai captures the imagination at Japan in EPCOT.

The variety of plants used by the Japanese in bonsai art is limited only by what is available. Even small-flowered, twiggy chrysanthemum varieties in a full range of colors (white, yellow, orange, and dark reds) are trained into erect cones as well as spreading, cascading, or forest groupings. Mums are dramatically trained to project from "lofty rock crags" with their exposed roots clinging to rock faces, stretching to the earth below.

A beautiful collection of bonsai trees is displayed on the front porch of the Yakitori House restaurant in EPCOT. The Oriental styling of the building was inspired by the tranquil architecture of the Katsura Imperial Villa in Kyoto and is a perfect setting for the diminutive treasures.

Gravel or dry gardens, made with sand, gravel, and rocks, are raked to symbolize various water-related conditions, like waves, calmness, and islands. The simplistic and metaphorical beauty of a gravel garden is a perfect example of the philosophy of "less is more." The abbreviation in style is carried even further, where little rocks can symbolize vast mountain ranges and small plants epitomize whole forests.

Japanese gardeners often describe their gardens using the word *shibusa.* Translated, shibusa connotes simplicity, elegance, good taste, nobility, truth, and restraint — words often used in reference to religion, art, human nature, and etiquette.

The flow of water keeps this deer scare in perpetual motion.

How To Make A Gravel Garden

Raked gravel forms soothing wave patterns.

What You'll Need

- ❑ White gravel
- ❑ Wooden dowel rake
- ❑ Bender board (optional)
- ❑ 1 or 2 large rocks
- ❑ Broom

Pull all weeds and plant material out of the area where you will be spreading the gravel.

Spread the gravel 4" to 6" deep in your selected location. You can use bender board to contain the gravel and give the garden flowing curves.

Oriental-style plantings surround this serene gravel garden at Japan in EPCOT.

3 Walk on the gravel to firmly pack it and add one or two large rocks for "islands."

4 Carefully sweep the gravel smooth with the broom and "draw" your "waves" with the wooden dowel rake.

Bamboos at Japan in EPCOT

A thick grove of Golden Bamboo *(Phyllostachys aurea)* stands in the gardens at Japan in EPCOT. This type of bamboo is cold-tolerant due to a specialized cross-bridging in the cell structure of the leaves. If you hold a leaf up to the light, you can easily see this intricate netting due to the large size of the cell walls.

The beauty of bamboo is equal to its durability and usefulness.

The Japanese use bamboo, known for its strength, durability, and flexibility, extensively in their architecture, in furniture making, in the preparation of daily meals, as well as in scaffolding for building construction.

You'll notice a bamboo-style railing as you walk over the small stream to the koi fish pond at Japan in EPCOT.

Common Plants for Oriental Gardens

Ajuga
Apricot
Bamboo
Bonsai
Cherry
China aster
Chinese wisteria

Crab apple
Dichondra
Dwarf mondo grass
Epimedium
Evergreen azalea
Formosan gum tree
Ginkgo tree

Golden rain tree
Japanese black pine
Japanese cedar
Japanese pagoda tree
Japanese painted fern
Maidenhair spleenwort
Maple
Mimosa
Moss

Plum
Privet
Quince
Sawleaf zelkova
Water lotus
Water lilies
Weeping cherry or birch
Wild ginger
Wintergreen
Yew

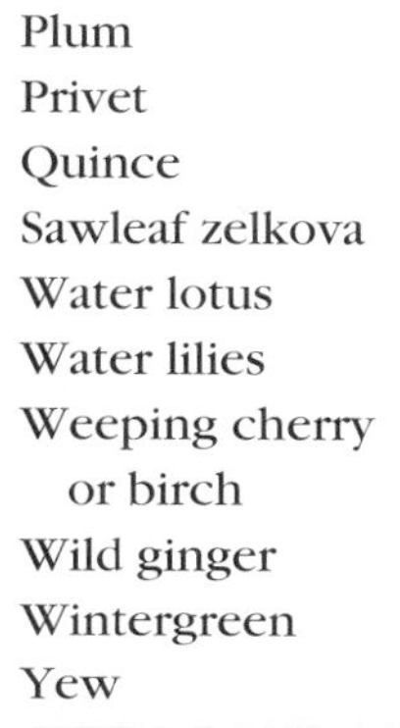

Cottage Gardens

Recreations of the nostalgic English country gardens have vast appeal for modern gardeners because they are beautiful, look natural, feature long-lived perennials perfect for indoor bouquets, and are relatively easy to maintain.

Cottage gardens, sometimes referred to as Shakespeare gardens, exude an air of carefree romance, with their watercolor-hued blossoms, inviting walkways, and an exuberant, anything-goes aura. These charming gardens are often comprised of climbing vines, antique roses, cobblestone courtyards, lattice fences, herb gardens, fruit trees, and an eclectic mix of annuals, vegetables, and shrubs.

Climbing vines furnish a bit of quaint character at **United Kingdom** *in* **EPCOT**.

In the early days, the wide variety of plants was grown not for decorative purposes, but to provide food, medicine, and household products likes lotions, cleansers, dyes, cosmetics, and insecticides.

Herbs grow in a formal knot garden at **United Kingdom** *in* **EPCOT**.

Stone edging is a natural choice for this winding path.

Though this homey garden style looks as if everything has grown of its own freewill, there really is a certain amount of planning involved to create the proper character. The easiest method is to create a simple plan, with free-flowing lines, and allow the multitude of plants to create the complexity and interest. Select and situate the plants so there will always be something happening — an ever-changing portrait of striking color, fragrant blossoms, and luxuriant growth.

Certain plants will self-sow themselves in some climate zones. Just allow the flowers to ripen, dry, and release their seeds to the soil. Over the winter, cold and damp weather will force the seeds to germinate for spring. Once the little seedlings have poked their way through the earth you can cultivate it, but not before. Soon after you'll be enjoying a whole new season of color.

United Kingdom in EPCOT embraces a number of English architectural styles. Each of the styles has its own special theme garden to match. The gardens vary from finely pruned boxwood hedges, parterres, and rose gardens to potted plants and informal hanging baskets adorning the village walk outside the shops. Adjacent to "Anne Hathaway's Cottage," a thatched roof replica of the home belonging to the wife of William Shakespeare, grows a perennial garden reflecting the type you might still find in the rural English countryside.

Common Cottage Garden Plants

Alyssum
Anemone
Apple
Lemon Balm
Bleeding Heart

Boxwood
Carnation
Chrysanthemum
Clematis
Columbine
Coreopsis
Cosmos
Crocus
Crown Imperial
Daffodil
Daisy
Dianthus

Fennel
Forget-me-not
Foxglove
Hawthorn
Helianthus
Hollyhock
Honeysuckle
Hosta
Hyssop
Ipomea
Iris
Ivy
Lamb's Ear
Laurel Bay

Lavender
Lupine
Madonna Lily
Marigold
Marjoram
Mint
Moonflower Vine

Myrtle
Pansy
Parsley
Peony
Periwinkle
Phlox
Poppy
Primrose
Rose
Rosemary
Rue
Sweet William
Thyme
Tulip
Verbena
Violet
Woodbine
Wormwood
Zinnia

Mickey's Favorite Perennials for the United Kingdom Garden in EPCOT

Avens *(Geum quellyon)*
Bachelor's Button *(Centaurea cyanus)*
Blue Daze *(Evolvulus nuttanllianus)*
Bush Daisy *(Euryops pectinatus)*
Butterfly Bush *(Ascelpias tuberosa)*
False Heather *(Cuphea hyssofolia)*
Firespike *(Odontonerna stricktum)*
Mexican Bush Sage *(Salvia leucantha)*
Musk Mallow *(Abelmoschatus moschatu)*
Persian Shield *(Strobilanthes dyerianus)*
Shrimp Plant *(Pachystachys lutea)*
Starcluster *(Pentas lanceolata)*
Texas Sage *(Salvia coccinea)*

Desert Gardens

Desert plants offer some of the most unusual garden silhouettes, most stunning flowers, and are often the simplest to care for. The mere existence of these plants in the harsh desert climate pays tribute to the evolutionary process, providing some with spherical "paddles" to conserve water and others with thorns to hinder herbivorous bandits from plundering them.

Gravel mulch underscores the desert theme of Big Thunder Mountain in Magic Kingdom Park.

Some people assume cactus are the only plants comprising a desert garden. In fact, a desert garden can include many easy-care, beautiful flowering plants, too. Not all climates are desert garden-friendly (especially the far north or the humid southeast), but many times a sunny courtyard can protect this unique garden from weather extremes.

For a true desert theme, try plantings of cacti and succulents combined with drought-tolerant wildflowers. Mulch with gravel for an appropriate finishing touch. Some avid desert gardeners opt to add a wagon wheel for effect.

Planting in containers allows you to move your plants to a safer environment if necessary. Remember, if your location gets more than 15" of rain a year, true desert plants will not survive.

Disney Desert Gardens

The Sonoran Desert, encompassing areas in Arizona, Texas, and New Mexico in the U.S., was the inspiration for the vegetation surrounding Big Thunder Mountain in Disneyland Park and the Magic Kingdom Park. The Frontierland attraction is planted in Southwest desert-style and composed of four distinct zones: Valley Floor Desert, Riparian Desert, Lowland Arizona Desert, and Highland Desert.

As Big Thunder Mountain Railroad careens up, over, through, and around Big Thunder Mountain, riders on the runaway train speed by desert areas landscaped with plants unique or similar to those found in each of the four areas.

The landscape at Big Thunder Mountain in Magic Kingdom Park respresents the U.S. Southwest's Sonoran Desert.

Mickey's Favorite Plants for Desert Gardens

Agave
Aloe
Barrel Cactus
Bear-Tongue
Beavertail

Coral Plant
Desert Christmas Cactus
Desert Spoon
Desert Willow
Elaeagnus
Giant Club Cactus
Golden Ball Cactus
Hall's Honeysuckle
Hedgehog Cactus
Jerusalem Thorn
Mesquite
Owl Eye Cactus

Pancake Pear
Pencil Cactus
Pencil Cholla
Peruvian Cactus
Prickly Pear
Rose
Saguaro Cactus
Slash Pine
Sweet Acacia
Staghorn Cholla
Teddy Bear Cholla
Texas Ebony
Texas Sage
Yaupon Holly

The Frontier Garden of Big Thunder Ranch

In the mid-1800s, when adventurous folk rolled their covered wagons westward, and settled the new frontier, their gardens were a lifeline to their existence. The main purpose of their gardens was to supply food, but also important were their herb gardens. Herbal remedies were necessary when a doctor was not available in the vast wilderness. Gardens also served as a visual reminder to their ties back home in the east.

A rustic picket fence keeps hungry "varmints" from raiding the Frontier Garden.

A frontier garden has been recreated in Disneyland Park at the Big Thunder Ranch house. The old-time garden includes carnations, strawflowers, sage, roses, thyme, oregano, parsley, lavender, rosemary, basil, yarrow, fennel, peppermint, chives, and apple trees.

Disneyland gardeners face many of the same pests, weeds, and animals that the early settlers encountered. They also use pest control methods similar to what was used back then, including hand-picking insects off the plants. No chemical controls are used on the Big Thunder Ranch because of the close proximity of the ranch animals, and because of the Disney commitment to using environmentally safe pest controls.

Tropical Gardens

A real tropical jungle is characterized by several "layers" of plants. The tallest layer is usually a canopy of trees filled with epiphytic orchids and bromeliads. Epiphytic plants get their support from the plants they attach themselves to, but no nutrients.

The next layer typically consists of smaller, vine-covered palms and trees, and finally an under-story layer of low-growing shrubs

and shade-tolerant plants. The overall effect is a lush curtain of greenery, punctuated by bright, colorful flower blossoms.

A tropical theme garden can be created in most climate zones or a sunny location indoors because there are many look-alike plants available. If you don't live in a sub-tropical climate, select plants native to your region that have a tropical appearance.

Exotic-shaped leaves or showy blossoms are preferable, as well as plants with leaves that are extraordinarily large and deep, glossy green. Climbing vines, bamboo, and banana palms can complement the jungle motif, too.

Many creatures find refuge in the tropical jungle of **Discovery Island.**

The tropical jungle at Mexico surrounding the pre-Columbian Mayan temple in EPCOT fittingly features a wide variety of lushly growing plants, including a silver trumpet tree, Mexican fan palm, orchid trees, bougainvillea, and exotic flowers.

A sharp turn onto a circular path takes you "deep into an over-grown jungle," where some brightly colored tropical birds and a Canary Island date palm add to the "authenticity."

The dry, arid tropical landscape of the Pacific Northwest region of Mexico is represented around the Cantina de San Angel. The plantings include a beaked yucca tree *(Yucca rostrata)* that is over 250 years old, night blooming cereus, and agave.

Mexico *in* **EPCOT** *is home for this colorful couple.*

The scenic Jungle Cruise in Disneyland and its sister attraction at the Magic Kingdom are perfect models of planned tropical gardens. The Adventureland attractions feature dense vegetative plantings, tangles of vines, colorful flowers, and winding rivers — not to mention, a whole gamut of snakes, hippos, zebras, elephants, rhinos, and headhunters! The Disneyland Park attraction also features realistic reproductions of Amazon rainforests.

The plants have been growing for over 40 years at the two and one-half acre Jungle Cruise in Disneyland Park.

A stream meanders through the lush foliage on Discovery Island.

Pleasure Island "adventurers" might meet a few new friends.

A canopy of ficus, bamboo, and palms tower 70 feet overhead adding to the realism, mystery, and intrigue of the attraction. Each night, sprinklers hidden in the treetops send a shower of water down onto the thirsty plants. So many plants are packed into the space that they all fiercely compete for water and nourishment.

The Caribbean Plaza in Adventureland in Magic Kingdom Park presents many elements of the 18th century New World Spanish Missionary gardens. The arched doorways, flowering trees, cascading bougainvillea, and hanging baskets add to the tropical ambiance.

The Indiana Jones™ Adventure Jungle

Indiana Jones, the courageous explorer popularized in the film trilogy created by George Lucas, was the inspiration for the Indiana Jones™ Adventure in Disneyland Park. Mysteriously concealed, deep within the dense jungles of Adventureland, lies the fabled Temple of the Forbidden Eye.

Guest explorers embark on a spine-tingling journey, encountering explosions, crackling fire, bubbling lava pits, ominous steam vents, a crumbling ceiling, shrieking mummies, rodents, sharp-fanged snakes, an avalanche of creepy crawlies, and confront the frightening temple deity herself.

To complement the jungle theme of the attraction, Disney gardeners selected a variety of tropical plants from South America, South Africa, Asia, Australia, and New Zealand.

The jungle includes African hemp, African tulip trees, anthurium, bamboo, bleeding coral trees, bromeliads, elephant ear plants, ginger plants, lychee nut trees, orchids, and puka trees. Some of the bamboo planted is expected to eventually reach 50'!

Purposely over-grown plantings provide the appropriate mysterious atmosphere.

© DISNEY/LUCASFILM LTD.

Common Plants for Tropical Gardens

Angel's Trumpet
Bamboo
Banana Palm
Banyan Tree
Begonia
Bougainvillea
Bromeliad
Bunya Bunya Tree
Caladium
Coral Tree
Croton
Elephant Ear
Eucalyptus
Ferns
Ficus
Floss Silk Tree
Gardenia
Hibiscus
Hoya multiflora
Impatiens
Ixora
Jacaranda
Kahili Ginger
Mexican Flame Vine
Orchid
Palm

Papyrus
Philodendron
Selloum
Princess Flower
Red Powderpuff
Scrambled Egg Tree
Shell Ginger
Shrimp Plant
Silver Trumpet Tree
Sky Flower
Trumpet Vine
Tupidanthus

Wildlife Gardens

Birds, butterflies, hummingbirds, and wildlife like deer and squirrels will feel welcome to your yard if you provide their three basic needs: food, water, and shelter.

Add a bird feeder or suet ball and watch your feathered guests come flocking. Trees and birdhouses provide safe nesting sites and fruit-bearing shrubs, like blackberry, raspberry, honeysuckle, viburnum, and pyracantha, supply additional food. Birds and butterflies are especially attracted to flowers like aster, daisy, marigold, verbena, and sunflower.

Butterflies and butterfly caterpillars also like a variety of wildflowers, weeds, herbs, and shrubs, including desert agave, borage, chickweed, coreopsis, white clover, nasturtium, parsley, plumbago, Queen Anne's lace, ragweed, thistle, and wisteria.

Hummingbirds are attracted to nectar-producing plants with orange or bright red tubular-shaped blossoms. Red pentas, red buckeye, coral bean, firebush, trumpet creeper, coral honeysuckle vines, and brightly colored annuals are also enticing to them. The dainty creatures enjoy a hummingbird feeder filled with sugar water, too.

Keep a birdbath, bowl, or a small pool filled with clean water to provide liquid refreshment to your wildlife. Frogs and turtles will enjoy the pond, and if you add a few rocks, reptiles and amphibians will be encouraged to join the crowd.

This little bunny doesn't realize some of the vegetation is off-limits.

Certain plants are natural attractants to butterflies and birds.

Theme Gardens for the Other Senses

Gardens aren't just for admiring with your eyes. Don't forget your other senses. You might enjoy a fragrance garden filled with alyssum, scented geranium, hyacinth, narcissus, lavender, peony, gardenia, lilac, rose, and clematis. Many gardeners like a garden filled with the sounds of windchimes, water, and the chirping of birds drawn by the plants and food provided to them. A theme garden of ornamental grasses offers a rich palette of textures, colors, heights, and even flower clusters.

Some gardeners create theme gardens around common edible flowers, using the beautiful petals, stems, and leaves to garnish salads, cakes, beverages, and entrees.

Edible plants include anise hyssop, basil blossoms, bee balm, borage blossoms, chive blossoms, lavender, marigold, nasturtium, pansy, pinks, sage blossoms, scented geranium, thyme blossoms, and violet.

Scented geranium is one of the many plants you can add to a fragrance garden.

A Theme Garden of Herbs

Herbs play a significant role in our everyday lives. They're used to spice up our foods, mend our wounds, heal our illnesses, calm our spirits, cleanse, soften, and scent our skin and hair, aid in our digestion, decorate our homes, and even entertain our cats.

Many of the spices we now take for granted were once considered valuable treasure, not available at any price. History reminds us that the New World was discovered by European explorers in search of new trades routes to the spice-producing areas of Asia.

In medieval times, gardeners devised intricate patterns of herbs, colored earth, and stones known as "knot gardens." Typically, formal herb gardens were planted in geometric shapes with crisscrossing paths.

A lovely knot garden of herbs grows behind United Kingdom in EPCOT.

Common Herbs and Their Uses

Anise — *Leaves for salads, seeds for pastries, cookies*

Basil, Sweet — *Leaves for tomato dishes, salads, pastas*

Borage — *Leaves for salads or pickling*

Burnet — *Leaves for salads, iced drinks, vinegar, butters*

Caraway — *Seeds for flavoring pickles, Brussels sprouts, cabbage, cookies, bread*

Catnip — *Leaves for tea or kitty playtime*

Chamomile — *Blossoms used for tea*

Chive — *Shoots for salads, cheese and egg dishes, gravies, soups*

Coriander/Cilantro — *Seeds for potpourris, to flavor beans, stews, sausage, pastries, leaves for fowl, meats, spicy sauces*

Dill — *Leaves or ripened seeds for chicken, fish, lamb dishes, sauces, salad dressings, breads, stews*

Fennel — *Leaves and seeds season cheeses, fish, vegetables, salads*

Garlic — *To season salads, poultry, meats, butters*

Lavender — *Flowers for garnish, oils, perfumes, potpourri, tea, baths*

Marjoram, Sweet — *Leaves to flavor meats (especially lamb), vinegars, casseroles, salads, cooked peas, beans*

Mint — *Leaves for garnish (especially mint juleps, iced tea), lamb dishes, jelly, fruit cocktails*

Mustard — *Seeds ground for spice, leaves for salads, vegetable dishes*

Nasturtium — *Leaves for cottage cheese, flowers for salads, pickled seeds for meat dishes*

Oregano — *Leaves to flavor meats, spicy foods, vinegars, casseroles, salads*

Parsley — *Stalks for garnish, leaves for tomato dishes*

Rosemary — *Leaves for vegetables, meat, chicken, or pork dishes, stew*

Sage — *Leaves to season lamb, poultry, sausage, stuffings*

Savory — *Leaves for fish, meats, eggs, beans, soups, vinegars, sausages, liqueurs*

Sweet Bay — *Leaves for spaghetti, meat loaf, stews*

Tarragon — *Leaves for fish, egg dishes, salads, vinegars, cheese, soups*

Thyme — *Leaves to season fish, poultry, meat, vegetables, stuffings, stews, vegetable juices, soups*

TRIVIA

- In their search for the Northwest Passage, European explorers opened up new trade routes throughout the world allowing botanists to collect seeds and plants from far away places. Conservatories, arboreta, and botanical gardens grew in popularity providing storage for foreign plants and a facility for research and education in botany and horticulture. The Victorian-style Crystal Palace in Magic Kingdom Park was designed after a conservatory at Golden Gate Park in San Francisco.

- At Morocco in EPCOT, the landscaping theme reflects the country's strong agricultural ties. Citrus trees, date palms, and bananas are among the useful plants found growing there. Across the promenade, an ancient waterwheel (an accessory typical to Moroccan life) provides irrigation water to channels that divide a raised garden. This traditional four-fold garden or "chahar bagh" is of Persian design.

- During the European Renaissance (1400-1700), Italian, French, and English gardens were formal in nature and strictly ornamental. They featured straight pathways, clipped hedges, balustrades, fountains, pools, and sculpture. Parterres were also an important feature of the Italian and French gardens. The patterned beds of alternanthera outside the Crystal Palace in Magic Kingdom Park were inspired by these elaborate formal gardens. Around 1700, the English had tired of formal geometric gardens and began to develop a more naturalistic and informal landscape style. Large expanses of green grass and rolling hills planted with trees surrounding picturesque lakes dominated English estates. The Hub area in Magic Kingdom Park is an example of this English gardening style.

- Disney Village Marketplace features a contemporary landscape style of California. This garden style was the creative solution to a fuel shortage in the 1930s. To encourage people to remain at home, outdoor living areas were designed to be both useful and attractive using various textures of paving materials and plants in new ways.

- In the late fall, when the leaves have fallen, the sycamore trees at Germany in EPCOT clearly show they have been "pollarded." A traditional European style of pruning, pollarding was a technique to grow and harvest kindling wood each year. At Walt Disney World Resort, the removal of small, whip-like branches each year form a limited number of knob-like stubs, creating a rounded appearance in the summer and a distinctive silhouette in the winter.

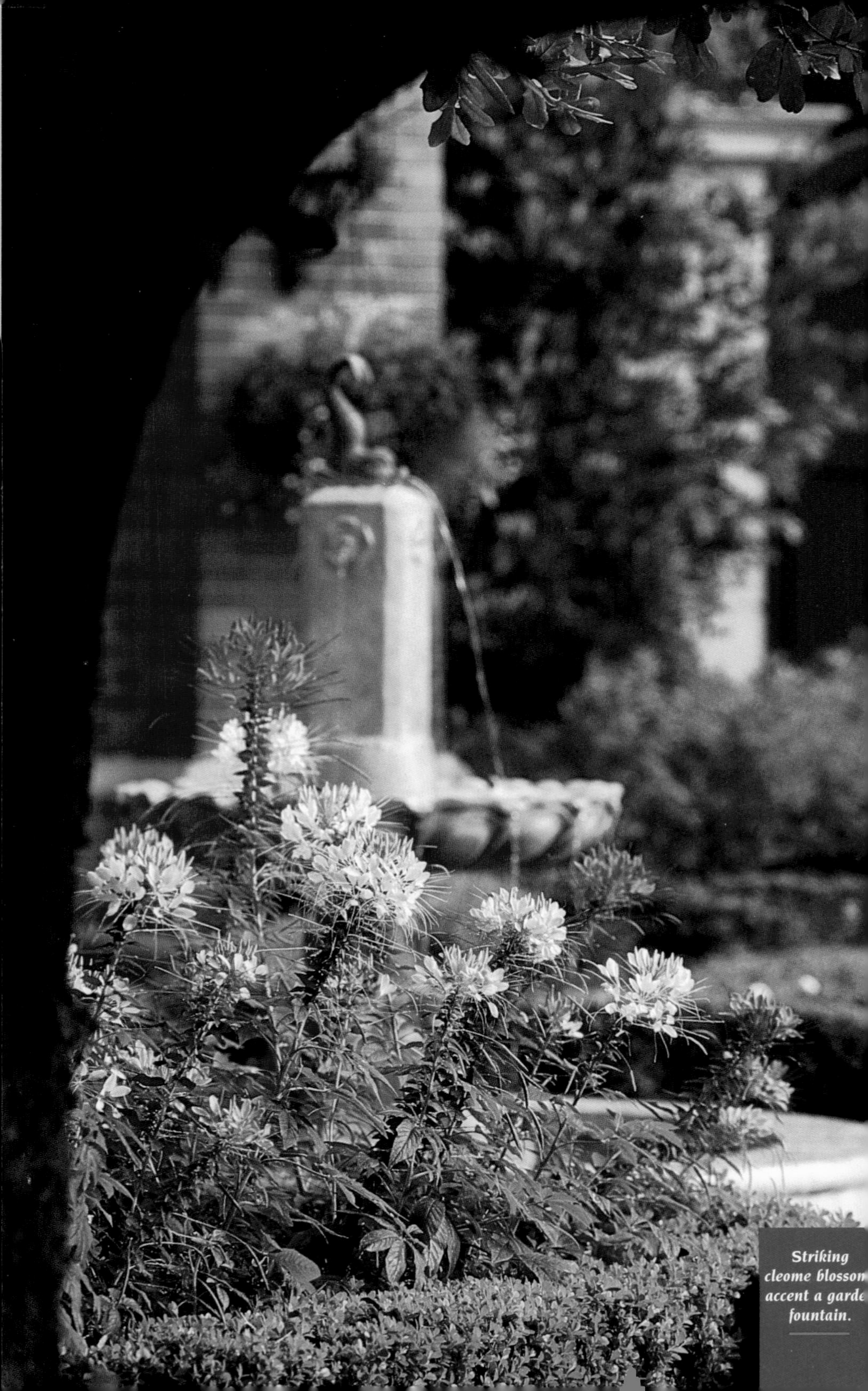

Striking
cleome blosson
accent a garde
fountain.

Imagine your landscape as a special outdoor room — an extension of your home. Now imagine that you're going to decorate your garden to make it more beautiful, comfortable, and entertaining. Think of the grass as carpeting; trees as the ceiling; bushes and fences as walls; paths as hallways; and flowers, statuary, planters, bird houses, and fountains as accessories or accents. These accents can help you tie your whole garden theme together.

An urn tops a wall in the arid oasis of Morocco in EPCOT.

The garden accents in Walt Disney Theme Parks and Resorts are carefully selected to coordinate with the themes of the surrounding areas. Statues, walkways, light fixtures, containers, fountains, seating areas, sculptures, and all the special features, enhance and reinforce the theme of each setting.

Old-fashioned lampposts and ornate Victorian benches are set along Main Street, U.S.A. Rusty train parts dot the desert landscape around Big Thunder Mountain Railroad. Blazing torch lamps light the paths at Disney's Polynesian Resort. Guests walk across a bouncy barrel bridge to visit Tom Sawyer Island in Disneyland Park. Tiki figures and temple "ruins" add atmosphere to the Jungle Cruise.

This gazebo is a tropical focal point at Disney's Caribbean Beach Resort.

Planning Your Garden Accents

Decorating your garden can be as simple and inexpensive as adding a lawn chair to your patio or as extravagant as building a pool, cabana, or outdoor kitchen.

Ask yourself what you enjoy doing in the yard (relaxing, exercising, dining, playing, entertaining, growing your own food,...). Do you need the enclosure, security, and privacy of a fence and gate or do you want you and your "furnishings" showcased for the viewing pleasure of all who drive by? Is there enough room for a big addition, like a gazebo or volleyball court, in the landscape? Or is your "landscape" a small balcony or deck you wish to beautify? Will you need to add electricity for new lighting or electrically powered enhancements?

What is your budget? If you have grand plans, but not enough cash to do it all at once, decide what is the most important and do that first. Think carefully, get competitive prices, then chart your course for future additions.

You'll find a wealth of ideas for landscape decorating at Walt Disney Theme Parks and Resorts, in home and garden magazines, catalogs, garden and patio stores, and in your own neighborhood.

This decorative lamp is attractive both day and night.

Mickey's Favorite Garden Accents

Arbors
Architectural stonework
Baskets
Benches
Bird baths, houses, and feeders
Bowls
Decorated pots
Edgings
Finials
Fountains
Gazebos
Pavilions
Pedestals
Seating areas
Statuary
Strawberry pots
Sundials
Tables
Trellises
Troughs
Urns
Vases
Wall plaques
Wind chimes

A raised deck offers a nice overview of the landscape at **Disney Vacation Cl**

Patios, Decks, and Other Seating Areas

At the Magic Kingdom Park, Adventureland guests relax on a tropical verandah overlooking water and lush, jungle-like plantings. Sleek, one-piece benches provide comfortable seating in Tomorrowland and underscore the futuristic landscape. Umbrella-covered chaises and beachfront "porch" swings grace Disney's Grand Floridian Beach Resort.

At the Treehouse Villas in Disney's Village Resort, story-high raised decks offer commanding views of the wooded setting. Café bistro chairs make perfect people-watching perches for visitors at France in EPCOT. In Disneyland Park, guests relax at tables and chairs in a quiet alcove in the *Fantasia* Garden.

Consider the location of your seating area carefully, particularly if you have a beautiful vista or an eyesore in the distance. If you will be using the area for dining, plan it close to the house so you won't have to cart the food and all the dining paraphernalia a long distance. Be sure to provide some shade with an umbrella, tree, or other overhead covering. A deck or patio facing west or south may heat up like a brick oven in the summertime.

Lush landscaping shades this ornate metal bench.

While you're planning, also remember that certain tiles and other surfaces can become hot enough to burn tender skin or become dangerously slippery when wet. Non-skid tiles and other materials that don't retain heat well are now available at building supply stores.

Patios and decks create level ground for furniture and planters and offer the most room-like look in outdoor decorating. Typically, people build patios and decks directly off a kitchen or family room, providing easy access to the outside. Sometimes the area is simply a concrete pad dressed up with flower-filled containers. Occasionally, people build elaborate multilevel-decks with a variety of seating options, built-in planter boxes, and railings all the way around. This last feature is important if your deck or patio is located on a steep grade.

All seating areas don't have to be located on a patio or deck. Be creative! Place a bench next to a fountain to enjoy the sight and the sound. Surround a table and chairs with colorful flowers. Hang a hammock from a stand and move it around the yard to suit your mood. Build a lofty treehouse and join the kids for some sky-high fun. Fasten an old-fashioned swing to a sturdy branch.

Statuary and Other Garden Decorations

Walt Disney Theme Parks and Resorts abound with interesting garden embellishments. For example, at Japan in EPCOT, a very special stone lantern welcomes guests. The lantern was presented to Roy O. Disney by the Japanese government to commemorate the opening of Walt Disney World in 1971.

Pluto stands guard below a cartoon-colored bird house at Mickey's Starland in Magic Kingdom Park.

Splash Mountain at Disneyland Park and Magic Kingdom Park features ornate wooden bird houses. A spectacular soaring statue representing the DNA molecule serves as a landmark at Wonders of Life in EPCOT. A contemporary sculpture near the entrance to EPCOT features its stylized logo. At night, the same sculpture glows with a brilliant luminescence thanks to some clever lighting techniques.

The popularity of garden decorations is rapidly increasing, as evidenced by the abundance of garden specialty catalogs and interesting garden accents currently available.

People are now spending more time relaxing in their yards and on their balconies and decks. Gardens continue to be favorite places for leisure-time activity. Seating and entertainment areas in the landscape are also getting renewed attention as gardens become important settings for social gatherings with family and friends. Gardening is a gratifying hobby for many who enjoy the visual and physical pleasures of their toil.

Accessories like bird houses, wall plaques, unusual containers, and sundials can all add to the ambiance of your environment. The pleasant sound of a wind chime on a breezy day,

An Oriental lantern looks right at home in this mossy setting.

A tiki sculpture enhances the South Seas atmosphere at Disney's Polynesian Resort.

the splashing of birds taking a bath, the aesthetic appeal of a graceful statue, the sight of a flag fluttering in the wind, or the bubbling waters of a fountain enhance a landscape's allure and delight the senses, too.

Selecting garden accents should be performed with as much thought as home decorating. Ask yourself, "What's missing? What would look nice? What would add to the overall effect?"

If you like cheerful sound in your environment, add a bird house, bath, or feeder to encourage birds to visit your yard. Hang wind chimes from a nearby tree branch or under the eaves where they can swing free and be heard easily when the breeze blows. Remember, most people prefer the low, melodic sounds of larger chimes than the high-pitched tones of smaller ones.

You can create an intriguing focal point in your landscape by nestling a statue among the greenery. Statuary come in a wide array of styles from amusing or lifelike animals and fish; to sweet-faced frolicking children; to freeform, abstract sculpture; to classic and formal period figures; to architectural "findings" like old columns and containers; to pieces distinctly Oriental, Italian, or French; and the list goes on.

Find permanent locations for your acquisitions by moving the pieces around in your environment until you find just the right spot.

Snow White Grotto in Disneyland Park

A wonderful surprise with a mysterious origin awaits guests exploring Fantasyland. Snow White Grotto, nestled in a hidden corner near Sleeping Beauty Castle, features white marble statues of Snow White and her seven dwarf friends.

The beautifully carved, carefully crated figures were delivered to the Disney Studio in 1961 from an anonymous Italian donor. Nothing more is known about them, the generous benefactor, or their talented sculptor.

White marble statues of Snow White and the seven dwarfs delight guests in Fantasyland.

It was decided the statues deserved a special setting to showcase their beauty, however, there was one "slight" problem. The statues, though flawlessly executed, were all the same size.

To compensate for Snow White's dwarf-sized stature, she was located high atop a waterfall providing the illusion that she is far off in the distance. The playfully posed dwarfs were situated at the foot of the waterfall at the pond near the wishing well, giving appropriate perspective to the scene. The idyllic, fairy-tale setting is further enhanced by the sound of Snow White's delicate voice singing "I'm Wishing."

Walkways and Steps

The paths and walkways in Walt Disney Theme Parks and Resorts are made of a wide variety of materials to create a certain impression or to match a theme. For example, a rustic boardwalk path takes guests through the Wilderness Swamp Trail. At United Kingdom in EPCOT, a cobblestone path of large, smooth stones winds its way through a colorful perennial garden. Small, flat rocks form a cobblestone walkway to The Golden Galleon shop in Adventureland in Magic Kingdom Park.

At Disney's Contemporary Resort, sidewalks feature bold directional graphics that make even better sense when viewed from several stories up — they point the way to and from the Resort! At Discovery Island, mulched paths take visitors through a lush jungle world of exotic animals, reptiles, and birds.

A floral motif decorates this staircase.

A walkway or path is one of the most important elements in a garden because it encourages exploration through the heart of the landscape, provides a safe, dry place for strolling, links one section of the grounds with others, protects the lawn and plants by winding around them, and makes the most of lovely vantage points if properly planned.

You don't need acres of land to create a nice walkway. In fact, your path could be a simple curve leading from the back door to the garage or a pebble-lined walk to the mailbox. Think about how you typically walk through your yard. You may not even realize you ramble along the same route each time. What a perfect spot for building a path!

A boardwalk path leads to a play area.

When selecting building material for your walkway or steps, take into consideration the mood you want to create, the slope of the land, whether or not the ground is wet in certain areas or at certain times, and how formal or informal and permanent you want the path to be. Remember that some materials require more maintenance.

For example, fieldstone and brick need occasional weeding; moss requires frequent watering; pine needles and bark chips may need yearly replenishing; a grass path needs mowing, watering, weeding, and feeding; and pressure-treated lumber or railroad ties eventually need to be replaced.

Most garden supply stores now carry pre-shaped concrete pavers in common geometric shapes, like circles, squares, and rectangles, and some are even designed to look like sea shells and flower blossoms. They are attractive, easy to install, and weather the elements well.

A strong foundation for your walkway and steps has many virtues. A 2" to 6" gravel or sand base will maintain the beauty and longevity of your efforts for years. Your walkway and steps will be less likely to sink into mud during rainstorms or buckle in freezing winter temperatures. A good sand or gravel base allows water to drain easily from under your paving materials, too.

How to Build a Fieldstone Path

What You'll Need

- ❑ Large, flat stones
- ❑ Trowel or sharp knife
- ❑ Shovel
- ❑ Sand

1. Select large, flat stones from a rock supply company or from your own property (if you're so lucky).

2. Position the stones along the grass in the pattern they eventually will follow.

3. One-by-one, outline their shapes in the soil using the trowel or knife, leaving the stones in place.

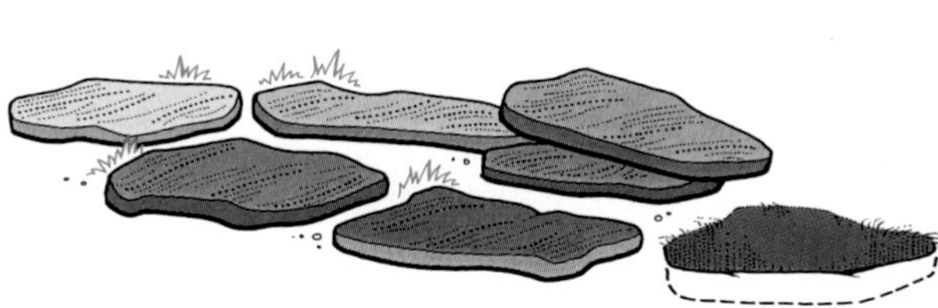

4. Lift the first stone and set it aside. Dig a hole deep enough to accommodate the depth of the stone and then dig down 2" farther.

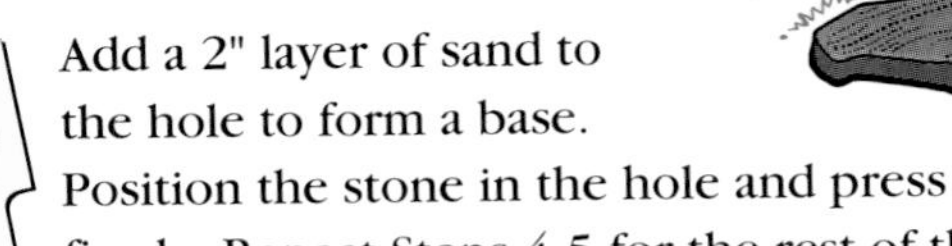

5. Add a 2" layer of sand to the hole to form a base. Position the stone in the hole and press firmly. Repeat Steps 4-5 for the rest of the stones.

Walls, Fences, and Gates

People add walls, fences, and gates to create a specific "look," provide privacy or security, obscure an unsightly view, keep kids and animals either in or out, add protection from prevailing winds, and sometimes to produce an illusion.

Fences and walls are made out of many materials and come in many styles: lacy peekaboo lattice, charming wooden picket, frilly Victorian scrollwork, stately and substantial metal, sturdy brick, rocks, utilitarian chain link, Spanish stucco, wooden panels or boards, and rough-hewn logs, to name a few. Trellises and screens can also become effective as fences and walls.

At Liberty Square in Magic Kingdom Park, a stone wall is complemented by nearby wrought iron lamps providing a Colonial impression. A curving tile-capped wall surrounds China in EPCOT and ornately patterned mosaic tile walls accentuate the theme in Morocco. In Disneyland Park, Walt Disney's monogram is discreetly woven into the iron balustrade at The Disney Gallery in New Orleans Square. Rugged split rail fencing befittingly surrounds Big Thunder Ranch, adding the right amount of "homestead" atmosphere.

Some fences and walls completely surround a property and others merely separate one part of the yard from another. Some are elegant and expensive and others are practical and modestly priced. Be sure the fence or wall you choose for your landscape is not overpowering in size and that it matches the style of your home. Also take maintenance into consideration.

If you paint or stain a fence once, you'll be painting or staining it many times in the years to come. You may then want to consider building with cedar and redwood. These two wood types naturally age to a mellow gray and never need to be painted or stained, however, wood is not as long-lasting as brick, metal, or cement.

Some people embellish their gates, walls, fences, and balconies by painting flowers or other decorative flourishes directly on the surfaces. Be sure to use exterior-quality paint if you decide to add artistic touches.

Delicate vines climb a stone wall at Canada *in* EPCOT.

You can create colorful camouflage on walls and fences by adding climbing plants, like roses, morning glory, bougainvillea, or wisteria. Planters can also be attached to walls and posts and filled with a mix of annuals and ivy for a really sensational look. The planters also break up long expanses of walls and soften their appearance. This is a fantastic option for apartment and condominium dwellers.

Gates often become an intriguing focal point accenting the fence or wall and sometimes even stand alone as an elegant sentry beckoning visitors. They are often designed to enhance an architectural style and can be massive enough to accommodate the entry of cars or small enough for neighborly visits from one yard to the next. Gates sometimes offer a small glimpse of what is beyond the entry with circular openings, peek holes, or strategically located slats.

Water Features

The sight and sound of water in a garden is a refreshing surprise. Water splashing upon rocks can sound like a musical waterfall. The reflection from a still pond can mirror the surroundings, doubling its beauty. A swimming pool can be a welcome oasis and a recreational focal point.

EPCOT *guests enjoy the beautiful landscaping and waterfront setting of* World Showcase Lagoon.

A fountain can bring vertical dimension to a horizontal landscape. A bridge or dock can create a perfect vantage point to admire water lilies, fish, sunrise or sunset. Adding water to your landscape may be as simple as installing a bird bath or small fountain.

Water, water everywhere.... During the opening ceremonies at EPCOT, the water from 20 countries was poured into the Fountain of Nations. A dramatic, modern sculpture arises from a wondrous fountain at Journey into Imagination in EPCOT. The watery sprays create a sparkling backdrop for the sculpture as it mimics the architectural angles of the glass and chrome pavilion.

A colorful, gigantic, serpentine slide deposits guests into a turquoise-blue pool at Disney's Port Orleans Resort. Mirrored tiles reflect the sunlight and azure-tiled pool fronting the Universe of Energy in EPCOT. A statue of St. George stands at the fountain pinnacle at the Biergarten entrance at Germany in EPCOT.

A playful fountain surprises visitors at Disney Village Marketplace.

Fountain water shoots up, creating a reverse waterfall at Journey into Imagination.

The Spanish-themed Fountain del Fortuna flows near Pirates of the Caribbean in Magic Kingdom Park. Log flume riders land in a briar-filled pond at Splash Mountain. A tranquil pond adds dignity and serene beauty at China in EPCOT. A pineapple-motif fountain symbolizes friendship near The Crystal Palace in Magic Kingdom Park. Rocks punctuate and sometimes symbolically enhance ponds at Canada, China, and Japan in EPCOT.

The sea god Neptune is immortalized in a lovely fountain setting at Italy, surrounded by container plantings and dense bougainvillea.

A topiary Mickey tops this fountain in Disney Village Marketplace.

Play Areas

Swing sets, monkey bars, teeter-totters, sandboxes, mini swimming pools, and the whole multitude of play areas are even more fun when appropriately landscaped. Consider locating the recreational areas in a place protected from the sun so the surface temperatures of these "toys" won't get scorching hot during the midday. In Disneyland Park, a large ficus tree provides shade and acts as a natural focal point in a Mickey's Toontown play area. Potted geraniums attached to light poles along the perimeter of the area accentuate its boundary.

Sand makes a soft "landing pad" in this play area.

You can keep a watchful eye on the activity if you locate your children's play area in plain view from the house. You might also want to frame the area with a small hedge, plant a shade tree, or add some flowers the kids could tend.

Do-it-yourself types can design their own play area or build one from a kit containing everything but the tools. Installing a sandbox can be as simple as digging a square hole 8" deep and filling it with clean sand. Add a couple pails and shovels and set the kids free! Many of the Walt Disney World Resorts, as well as Typhoon Lagoon and River Country, feature fun-filled sandy play areas for children of all ages.

If you're exceptionally handy or know a carpenter with a sense of humor, you might build a pint-sized duplicate of your home as a cozy playhouse for the kids. Dwarf-sized bushes, a couple of small trees, and a tiny flower garden will add a touch of whimsy to the scene. The kids will get years of enjoyment out of their hideaway and when they outgrow it, you can utilize the space as a storage area.

A tent can become a favorite clubhouse for kids.

A floral arch and topiary maze welcome young guests in Mickey's Starland.

If you're really creative, add a kid-sized topiary maze to your play area. In Mickey's Starland, the "Mouse-ka-Maze," an annual-topped labyrinth, tempts and delights young Magic Kingdom visitors.

Play areas are not just for kids anymore. Some "playful" adults are setting aside yard space for tennis, volleyball, and badminton courts, as well as workout stations. If the idea of viewing these areas from inside doesn't appeal to you, plant some fast-growing shrubs or add a trellis to conceal the view. You may want to add a bench and tree to shade spectators or as a place to take a break.

Bamboo-shaped lights accent an Oriental theme.

Outdoor Lighting

Nighttime brings a rich, new dimension to Walt Disney Theme Parks and Resorts. Twinkling lights outline boats, buildings, piers, and parade floats. Spotlights dramatically accentuate trees, architectural features, walkways, and illuminate nighttime shows. Laser lights slice through the evening sky and fireworks explode with a pyrotechnic fury. Subdued lighting safely guides guests along the sidewalks and softly glowing fixtures of every different kind and shape welcome them through Disney doorways.

Colored lights make fountains gush in muted tones and buildings take on all new palettes. Shimmering lights reflect from ponds, pools, lakes, and rivers. Ghostly light creates spooky shadows and eerie effects at The Haunted Mansions and The Twilight Zone Tower of Terror™. Soft pastel lights turn fairy-tale castles into magical palaces.

Lighting expands the time you can enjoy your outdoor areas, provides safety, produces unusual special effects, beautifully spotlights planted areas for nighttime viewing, and can create special landscape moods.

We're fortunate to live in a time when visual appeal, rather than merely function, is given special consideration in lighting design. Contemporary outdoor lighting is so much more than a glaring spotlight harshly illuminating the driveway. There are strings of hanging lanterns, accent lights in the shape of elegant art nouveau flowers, colored spotlights, lights created just for walkways, decks, and docks, recessed lighting, pool lighting, movement-sensitive security lighting, and timed lighting. There is even a whole profession collectively known as Lighting Consultants and Designers to help us sort this all out.

Plants, water, and architecture are beautifully illuminated at China in EPCOT.

tic lanterns hang from hewn log poles at Canada in EPCOT.

Throughout Walt Disney Theme Parks and Resorts, the lighting and light fixtures help enhance the themes. For example, strings of hanging lanterns add a festive touch to the landscape at Japan in EPCOT. On Main Street, U.S.A., old-fashioned lampposts, adorned with hanging baskets, glow softly in the evening, setting the scene for a turn-of-the-century feeling. Tiny white lights glitter in trees throughout Disney Village Marketplace year 'round.

Lighting can add a new dimension to any evening landscape. A light situated at the base of a tree pointing up the trunk and into the branches produces interesting shadows and silhouettes. A set of low-voltage lights lining a walkway is inviting and offers safe passage to visitors strolling the path. At night, a swimming pool takes on a bewitching turquoise glow with subtle underwater lighting. A softly radiating lamppost near the end of your drive serves as a welcoming marker on a dark street.

TRIVIA

- The dark water at China in EPCOT is one of the most highly regarded features in the garden, serving as a canvas for reflection of the landscape and architecture. It has been said that a Chinese garden without water looks like a face with its eyes closed.

- At Big Thunder Ranch in Disneyland Park, whiskey barrels contain culinary herbs, an old-fashioned wheelbarrow holds tools, and an egg basket cradles begonias.

- The garden at Italy in EPCOT features a collection of terra-cotta pots filled with flowering plants for a patio garden ambiance. Garden statuary is used as a focal point, while hanging baskets bring the color to eye level. Their textures and soft colors complement the "Old World" aura of the Italian Renaissance.

- You'll notice interesting rocks used throughout the China garden in EPCOT. Large or oddly shaped rocks were a common element in Imperial gardens and the most desirable stones were of limestone with deep holes, the result of years of gradual erosion.